THE ULTIMATE 80s KITCHEN ENCORE

POP LIFE

THE ULTIMATE 80s KITCHEN ENCORE

POP ICON

Tiffany

&

CELEBRITY CHEF

Alicia Shevetone

Pop Life: The Ultimate 80s Kitchen Encore

ISBN Hardcover - 978-1-968919-13-9
Paperback - 978-1-968919-15-3
eBook - 978-1-968919-14-6

Armin Lear Press, Inc.
215 W Riverside Drive, #4362
Estes Park, CO 80517

The book is dedicated to our grandmothers:

MIMI, SITO, MADELINE AND BARBARA

CONTENTS

BORN TO ROCK

VIP MEET & GREET

BACKSTAGE FOR THE BAND

AFTER PARTY

VEGAS RESIDENCY

SAHARA
Mexican Cuisine
Pop-Up Experience
SAHARA
STATUS
THE SPACE
CHEF ALICIA
PRESENTS
AN EVENING WITH TIFFA

READY TO POP

Welcome to Pop Life! Tiffany and Chef Alicia here. Two California girls. One, a multi-platinum recording artist and foodie. The other, a high-powered executive turned chef. We're an exceptional team! Tiffany brings the heart and the radio hits from her life: road snacks, mall-food memories, and home-pantry hacks that still work. Chef Alicia brings the craft: refined cuisine, confident technique, and presentation that feels special.

Pop Life isn't just a cookbook—it's part reference manual and part backstage pass for anyone who's ever wished they could remix the soundtrack of their lives. It's a delicious trip back to the 80s, where every recipe brings back memories of family gatherings, friends, and the flavors only we 80s kids know how to celebrate. Get ready for childhood snacks rebooted, zhuzhed-up comfort food, and glammed-up food court classics, all joyfully grounded in the present.

When you make these dishes, plate them like you mean it. Give them the stage.

OPENING ANNOUNCEMENTS

We've structured *Pop Life* like a duet, so you'll always know which voice is leading, and when the harmony kicks in.

TIFFANY introduces every chapter. *Her notes look like this.*

CHEF ALICIA walks you through the recipes, with Tiffany's liner notes woven throughout. *Her notes look like this.*

Each chapter also includes **CHEF'S TIPS** and a **BACKSTAGE TAKEAWAY**, which are concise notes from Chef Alicia designed to help you cook with confidence, anticipate common challenges, and refine your technique. Think of them as practical cues that will make your results consistent, professional, and effortless.

And now, the setlist begins, starting with the roots that made Tiffany Born to Rock. From there, VIP Meet & Greet serves up bite-size showpieces fit for mingling. Taking it to the bridge, Backstage for the Band fuels the long nights with bold, comforting flavors that keep everyone going. Then, After Party drops the beat with sweets, snacks, and late-night bites. Next, wind down with Vegas Residency and Chef Alicia's delectable dishes for two. Pop Lifestyle takes it beyond the kitchen—into fashion, cocktails, spices, and wellness—everything you need to pop, every day. And finally, the curtain rises again with Encore: Bonus Track, a *Teen Beat*-style Q&A and Tiffany's exclusive *Pop Life* single, just for you.

The house lights are dimming. The curtain is rising. You've got an awesome seat with a killer view. Let's start the show!

Born to Rock

- MEXICAN CHICKEN POT PIE
- CORNMEAL CASSEROLE MUFFINS
- ROASTED RED PEPPER RELISH
- HUMMUS WITH ZA'ATAR AND HOT HARISSA CHICKEN MEZZE PLATTER
- BEEF AND SOY WITH SHISHITO PEPPERS AND POCKY CRUNCH
- PIGGIES IN A BLANKET STUFFED WITH MAC & CHEESE
- CHEEZY CHICKEN NUGGETS
- LEBANESE CINNAMON CHICKEN SALAD
- TAMALE PIZZA
- MIMI'S MINI GERMAN CHOCOLATE MUFFINS
- SPINACH PIES

Growing up outside East LA in Norwalk, California, the kitchen was the heart of the family. My father is Lebanese, and his mother was best friends with my mom's mom, who was German. There were always tons of vibrant people in my grandma's home. My mom's favorite food was Mexican, which she learned to cook—sauces and all—from the Avon woman. Yes, this was the 80s, and the Avon woman was more than a makeup expert. She became a quick family staple, coming once a week to sell products and then, in the kitchen with a cup of coffee or a glass of tea, teaching my mom Mexican dishes.

We always gathered on Friday nights in the kitchen, as my family chain-smoked and played dominoes. There were tamales, stuffed grape leaves, fried chicken, biscuits and gravy, enchiladas, sausage, and sauerkraut; it was an array of foods all the time. As a kid, I just thought that's how it was.

My favorite time was after school when my mom made me special snacks. Chicken pot pies, mac and cheese, grilled cheese and tomato soup. It was never just a quick cold sandwich, because I ate those at school. Sometimes, if I was lucky, I could get the hot meal. We used to save up for those, so that was a special thing back in the 80s. But my mom still made me a hot snack when I came home. It was our thing, and it was one of my favorite childhood memories.

Three or four hours before dinner, we could play outside until the streetlights came on and then had to come home. It bridged that gap from school to homework to playing outside. I was a tomboy and a BMXer. I loved to climb trees, do crazy stunts on my roller skates and bikes. And I worked up an appetite. Having that after-school food (something special, some of my favorites) was everything. It could be a hot pocket-style snack, which my mom actually made from scratch.

My family wasn't big on buying pre-made food. My mom said, "We can always save money, and I can make it," and she was right. She made it better than the packaged meals, but I begged for the packaged food because it was the cool thing you saw in commercials. Those freezer pizzas? Of course, my mom would make them from scratch, and I remember arguing, "Why can't I be like the rest of the kids and just get the frozen pizzas?" But it was fun.

In addition to being a stay-at-home mom taking care of two kids, my mom always made big dinners. I laugh now when I look back, because going out to a sit-down family restaurant, even ordering takeout, was a special deal, for special occasions. The whole family would gather, and those nights felt golden. My family also threw a lot of parties at home or at local parks, where we'd grill and everybody brought a dish. Back home, my grandma's Norwalk kitchen smelled like garlic, onions, and whatever my grandma decided needed "just a little more" of both.

As I started to travel early in my career, most of the time, it was too expensive for my parents to come with me. I often went with someone from my label, experiencing all these different cultures away from my family.

My Norwalk high school had a diverse array of kids, but now I was suddenly in England, Germany, Japan, Thailand, and India. I didn't really know how to express everything I was seeing. It was hands-on experience and bigger than life. I always took pictures of the food. I've always been that original foodie taking pictures. But photos don't always pinpoint the culture, the vibrancy of the people, and their choices. Music does, but I found food was a great way to communicate the vibrancy and uniqueness of a region.

When I'd return to Norwalk, my grandma always let me experiment in her kitchen. By 16 or 17, I was in my mom's kitchen, my other grandma's kitchen, my auntie's kitchen, or even friends' kitchens, trying to replicate those dishes I had eaten abroad for my family. Finding ingredients like lemongrass in Norwalk was difficult, so I kept making things (cutting up limes, whatever I had) until I got close to the taste. Sometimes my family would say, "I'm not sure I like this. This is different." I remember my dad saying, "I don't really think I like curry. I don't know much about it." But he loved it, and he ate it.

Proving them wrong was fun, because I'd been the same way. A lot of times when faced with a new food, you think, "No, that's too weird. I won't like it." Then you taste it, and it's amazing. When I was in other countries, I'd often think, "I don't know if I'll like that," but I didn't want to be disrespectful, so I tried it anyway. In many cultures, food is the heart of things, and I learned early that saying no, or not trying something, can be extremely rude. There were things I wasn't sure I wanted to try, but I pushed myself, and I was proven wrong many, many times.

There are plenty of things I don't love. I'm not crazy about milk products. Fish can be iffy for me. I struggled with Japanese food; I never really mastered sushi, although my best friend is Japanese.

But I'd make the soups and noodles. I remember my first experience with live shrimp on the grill in Japan. It was scary. But I put on my game face, and it was very good.

So, I experienced the world on my own and brought it back to my family by recreating the dishes I discovered overseas. That's been a constant joy for me and something I love sharing with my fans now.

Food has always been around me. I learned that it gathers people, makes people happy, and brings different cultures together. It's always been in my blood, something I love so very much. This book is a setlist of those roots: everyday ingredients you still find on store shelves, reimagined into recipes that shine a little brighter with a touch of zhuzh.

Choosing the photos for this book made me misty-eyed. I saw my family albums: hands on pots, sleeves dusted with flour, tables crowded with cousins. You can't go back, but you can plate the memory and share it with friends.

That's the feeling I want you to have when you cook these dishes.

That's exactly what the Born to Rock recipes are about. They're the flavors of my childhood—Lebanese, German, Mexican, and pure 80s Americana—turned up with a little attitude. Some of my favorites were the hot snacks my mom made just for me after school. I think of them as my "After School Specials," that quiet pocket of time when it was just the two of us before the noise of the evening rolled in. Dishes like Mexican Chicken Pot Pie, Cheezy Chicken Nuggets, and Tamale Pizza all come from that warm, nurturing place.

I'll also share the foods that crowded our Friday-night table, from Spinach Pies and Cornmeal Casserole Muffins to Piggies in a Blanket stuffed with mac and cheese. Some dishes are rooted in my family's heritage—like Lebanese Cinnamon Chicken Salad and Mimi's Mini German Chocolate Muffins—while others echo the mash-up of cultures I tasted on the road, like the Roasted Red Pepper Relish, Beef and Soy with Shishito Peppers and Pocky Crunch, and the Hummus and Hot Harissa Chicken Mezze Platter covered in za'atar. Together, they make a playlist of the meals that raised me: comforting, bold, a little unexpected and totally ready to rock.

CHEF'S TIPS—BORN TO ROCK

Many of the recipes in this chapter involve bold flavors and layered textures—a combination that rewards patience and precision. These notes will help you avoid common pitfalls and get consistent results.

1. PERFECT BAKE = CLEAN SLICES

Applies to: Mexican Chicken Pot Pie, Cornmeal Casserole Muffins, Tamale Pizza

Thicken fillings before baking to prevent soggy layers. Bake just until golden and allow dishes to rest before cutting. This helps the structure set for neat, clean slices every time.

2. SEASON IN LAYERS

Applies to: Lebanese Cinnamon Chicken Salad, Roasted Red Pepper Relish, Hot Harissa Chicken Mezze Platter

Add seasoning gradually and taste as you go. If you're sensitive to heat, balance spice with a touch of sweetness (such as honey or agave) or a splash of acid (like citrus juice or vinegar).

3. MANAGE MINI PORTIONS

Applies to: Mimi's Mini German Chocolate Muffins, Piggies in a Blanket Stuffed with Mac & Cheese, Spinach Pies

One-bite and two-bite dishes bake quickly. In addition to watching your kitchen timer as dishes bake, lean into your senses of smell and sight. Watch for color and texture cues. When an aroma first wafts from the oven, you'll know small-format dishes are close to done.

4. KEEP CRISP AND CRUNCH DISTINCT

Applies to: **Cheezy Chicken Nuggets, Beef and Soy with Shishito Peppers and Pocky Crunch**

Maintain texture by letting fried or baked items rest on a wire rack. Add toppings or garnishes just before serving to preserve crunch.

5. STAGE INGREDIENTS BEFORE YOU BEGIN

Applies to: **Mexican Chicken Pot Pie, Hot Harissa Chicken Mezze Platter, Piggies in a Blanket Stuffed with Mac & Cheese**

These recipes have multiple components that come together quickly once cooking begins. Measure and prepare all ingredients in advance—from chopped vegetables to spice blends—so you can move smoothly through each step without overlooking details or overcooking any element. This practice is known as mise en place, a culinary term meaning "everything in its place."

BACKSTAGE TAKEAWAY

Focus on control for heat, moisture, and timing. These recipes reward careful preparation and confident seasoning over speed or improvisation.

When I was a kid, pot pie was the go-to after-school snack:
warm, flaky, and always waiting. Growing up in East LA, I
developed a serious love for heat, even though my family never
quite caught the spice bug. So naturally, I started dousing those
cozy little pies with Tapatio or whatever hot sauce I could find,
and just like that, the Mexican pot pie was born.

MEXICAN CHICKEN POT PIE

SERVES 8

There's something universal about wrapping familiar flavors in pastry. It feels celebratory, indulgent, and comforting all at once. This pot pie takes a classic American staple and layers it with Mexican inspiration: tender chicken, sweet corn, carrots, potatoes, and a hint of taco seasoning. Each bite is creamy and hearty, the perfect blend of homestyle comfort and festive flair.

INGREDIENTS

2 ears of fresh corn, husked and cleaned

4 large carrots

1 pound 4 ounces (566 grams) chicken tenders

2 tablespoons taco seasoning

1 tablespoon garlic powder

Salt and pepper, to taste

1/2 cup instant chicken gravy

1 1/4 cups unpeeled yellow potato, diced into 1/4-inch (roughly 0.5 cm) pieces

4 sheets frozen puff pastry, thawed

2 cups shredded cheddar cheese

Chopped cilantro or green onion, for garnish

INSTRUCTIONS

1. Preheat oven to 400°F (204°C).
2. Fill a large pot with 8–10 cups of water. Place the cleaned corn cobs and whole carrots into the pot. Bring to a boil over medium-high heat, then cover and cook for 15–20 minutes until just tender. This will create a light vegetable broth.
3. While the vegetables cook, place the chicken tenders in a skillet with about 1 cup of water. Season lightly with salt and pepper. Cover and cook over medium heat for about 15 minutes, or until the chicken is fully cooked all the way through and no pink remains. Remove the chicken from the pan, cool slightly and shred it into bite-sized pieces. Reserve the cooking liquid; set aside.
4. Transfer the cooked carrots to a cutting board and dice them into 1/4-inch (roughly 1/2 cm) cubes.
5. Cut the kernels off the corn cobs with a sharp knife; discard the cobs.
6. In a large sauté pan, add the diced carrots, corn kernels, 1–2 tablespoons of water, taco seasoning, garlic powder, and a pinch of salt. Cook over medium heat for 2–3 minutes, stirring occasionally.
7. Add the shredded chicken, the reserved broth, instant chicken gravy, 2 cups of water, and the diced potato to the pan. Stir well to combine. Simmer, uncovered, over medium heat for about 15 minutes, until the potatoes are fork-tender.
8. On a floured surface, roll puff pastry to 12 × 12 inches (roughly 30 × 30 cm). Cut pastry into 4 equal squares.
9. Lightly oil four 10-ounce (roughly 295 milliliters) oven-safe ramekins. Press a pastry square into each ramekin to form a shell. Trim away excess pastry. Use a fork to poke small holes in the bottoms of the pastry to promote even baking.
10. Spoon the chicken and vegetable mixture evenly into each ramekin, then top with a sprinkle of cheddar cheese.
11. Bake for 20–25 minutes until the pastry is golden and the filling is visibly bubbling.
12. Remove from the oven and let cool slightly before serving.
13. To serve, garnish with fresh cilantro or green onion.

CORNMEAL CASSEROLE MUFFINS

MAKES 48
MINI MUFFINS

There's a reason cornbread feels like it belongs everywhere: it's endlessly adaptable. These little muffins take that idea and give it a pop-star upgrade: tender cornbread bites that are soft, golden, and perfectly portioned for sharing. A little sweet, a little savory, and totally crowd-pleasing, they're the kind of food that vanishes as soon as they hit the table. And do yourself a favor: slather them with the Roasted Red Pepper Relish (recipe on page #)!

INGREDIENTS

1/2 cup corn kernels, fresh or canned and drained

1 can (14.75 ounces or 1 3/4 cups) creamed corn

1/2 cup jarred roasted red peppers, drained and chopped finely

1/4 cup jalapeños, seeded and minced finely (substitute green bell pepper if you don't want spice)

2 large eggs, beaten

1/3 cup unsweetened almond milk

1/4 cup olive oil

1 box (8.5 ounces or 240 grams) cornbread muffin mix

1/2 teaspoon onion powder

1/4 teaspoon garlic powder

1/2 teaspoon black pepper to taste

3/4 cup all- purpose flour (to flour muffin tin)

INSTRUCTIONS

1. Preheat oven to 375°F (190°C). Lightly grease two 24- cup mini muffin pans with oil or cooking spray, then dust each cavity lightly with all- purpose flour, tapping out any excess.
2. Place corn kernels and creamed corn in a bowl. Pulse with an immersion blender or food processor until slightly crushed.
3. In a large mixing bowl, combine creamed corn, corn kernels, 1/2 cup roasted red peppers, 3 tablespoons jalapeños, eggs, almond milk mixture, and olive oil.
4. Fold in the cornbread mix, onion powder, garlic powder, and black pepper until just combined. Do not overmix or the muffins may turn dense.
5. Spoon the batter into the muffin cups, filling each about 3/4 of the way full.
6. Bake in the preheated oven for 15–18 minutes, or until the muffins are golden on top and a toothpick inserted into the center comes out clean. Repeat this step for the remaining 24 muffins, if baking separately.
7. Let the muffins cool in the pan for 5 minutes before removing.

This one's got a fun little pop and bite that always takes me back to that warm, Southern kind of love. It's the kind of dish that's just as fun to make with your kids as it is to devour next to a big, creamy scoop of mac and cheese. A little tradition, a little twist. Comfort food at its finest.

ROASTED RED PEPPER RELISH

MAKES ABOUT 1 CUP

Bold, sassy, and smoky, this relish is one of those recipes that feels bigger than the sum of its parts. Just a handful of ingredients turns into something you'll want to put on everything: sandwiches, grilled meats, and especially Cornmeal Casserole Muffins (page 12). It's simple, keeps well in the fridge, and adds a pop of color and flavor wherever it lands.

INGREDIENTS

3/4 cup jarred roasted red peppers

1 1/2 teaspoons olive oil

1/2 teaspoon balsamic vinegar

1/4 teaspoon smoked paprika

Pinch of salt

INSTRUCTIONS

1. Finely chop the roasted red peppers and place them in a small bowl.
2. Add the olive oil, balsamic vinegar, smoked paprika, and a pinch of salt.
3. Stir everything together until well combined.
4. Let the relish sit at room temperature for at least 10 minutes to allow the flavors to meld.
5. Serve right away, or cover and refrigerate in an airtight container for up to 4 days. Bring to room temperature before serving for the best flavor.

This roasted Red Pepper Relish is a gem from Chef Alicia: simple, vibrant, and packed with flavor. It's the kind of recipe that instantly upgrades anything you pair it with, from apps to mains. A little sweet, a little smoky, and all thanks to Chef Alicia's expert touch.

HUMMUS WITH ZA'ATAR AND HOT HARISSA CHICKEN MEZZE PLATTER

SERVES 4

This scrumptious mezze platter reminds me of the Mediterranean menu we served the VIPs at our first event together in Las Vegas. For an extra chef-y twist, you can grill your lemon slices to caramelize the edges and add a subtle smoky depth to the dish. And if you really want to amp it up, serve this with a side of Tabbouleh (page 134).

INGREDIENTS

For hummus with za'atar:

6.4 ounces (roughly 180 grams) plain hummus

1/4 cup za'atar seasoning blend + additional for garnish

Olive oil, for drizzling

Fresh mint sprigs

1/2 teaspoon coarse salt

For harissa chicken baste:

1 tablespoon dried harissa

1 tablespoon olive oil

1/2 tablespoon lemon juice

1/4 cup tomato paste purée

1 pound (453 grams) chicken tenders

For assembly and serving:

1 cucumber, sliced

1 bundle radishes, ends trimmed

10 cherry tomatoes, halved

5 green olives

5 Kalamata olives

5 tabasco peppers (from pepper sauce or pickled, or jarred)

2 pepperoncini (pickled or jarred) peppers

10 cubes Parmesan cheese

3 lemon slices

INSTRUCTIONS

Hummus with Za'atar:

1. In a small mixing bowl, combine the hummus with 1/4 cup za'atar. Stir until evenly blended.
2. Transfer to a serving bowl and smooth the surface with a spoon.
3. Drizzle lightly with olive oil.
4. Finish with a light sprinkle of za'atar.
5. Garnish with fresh mint sprigs.

Harissa Chicken Baste:

1. In a small bowl, combine tomato paste, coarse salt, harissa, olive oil, and lemon juice.
2. Stir until the mixture forms a smooth paste.
3. Baste the chicken tenders evenly with the mixture.
4. Cook chicken with your method of choice until the internal temperature reaches 165°F (74°C):
   - Thread chicken onto skewers, grill 6–8 minutes per side over medium-high heat.
5. - Bake: 25–30 minutes at 400°F (204°C).
   - Air Fry: 18–20 minutes at 375°F (190°C).

Assembly and serving:

1. Place the bowl of hummus in the center of a large serving platter.
2. Arrange the cucumber slices, radishes, cherry tomato halves, olives, tabasco peppers, pepperoncinis, and Parmesan cubes around the hummus.
3. Add the cooked harissa chicken to the platter and garnish with lemon slices.

This one's pure magic on a platter: creamy hummus swirled with
za'atar and paired with hot harissa chicken that you can
grill, bake, or air fry. It's bold, herby, and effortless. If you've
purchased my Rock Star Za'atar and Hip Hop Harissa spice
blends, this is the perfect time to use them! Together they're the
best of both worlds: my Lebanese roots on one side, summertime
party vibes on the other. And just like a good set list, the combo
always leaves people wanting more.

This one takes me straight back to my days in Japan, where I did a commercial for Pocky, and I've been hooked on that flavor ever since. It's got that perfect graham cracker vibe, paired with rich dark chocolate that's not too sweet. And when you pair it with beef? Divine. The contrast just hits all the right notes, every time.

POCKY CRUNCH BEEF AND SHISHITO SKEWERS

SERVES 6

This dish combines East Asian flavor with a playful crunch. Thin-sliced beef is marinated with soy and ponzu, paired with blistered shishito peppers, and finished with a surprising garnish of sesame and crushed Pocky sticks—thin, chocolate-dipped cookie sticks popular in Japan. The result is bold, savory, smoky, and whimsical, a dish that feels sophisticated, yet fun.

INGREDIENTS

1 pound 4 ounces (566 grams) beef, sliced thinly

3 tablespoons ponzu sauce

1/3 cup soy sauce

3 tablespoons minced garlic

20 shishito peppers

1 lemon, juiced

2 1/2 teaspoons coarse salt

1/4 cup white sesame seeds

2 tablespoons vegetable oil

8–10 chocolate Pocky sticks, cut into 1/4-inch (roughly 1/2 cm) pieces, then crushed

20 4-inch (10 cm) bamboo skewers

INSTRUCTIONS

1. Place sliced beef into a resealable plastic bag. Add ponzu, soy sauce, and garlic. Seal and gently massage the marinade into the meat. Marinate at room temperature for 1 hour.
2. While beef marinates, wash and dry the shishito peppers. Place in a bowl and toss with oil until lightly coated.
3. Preheat a grill pan, griddle, or outdoor grill to high heat.
4. Place peppers on the hot grill. Squeeze lemon juice directly over them and sprinkle with salt. Cook 2–3 minutes on one side until blistered, then flip and cook another 2 minutes. Remove from heat and cut each pepper in half, crosswise, keeping the stems intact.
5. Spread sesame seeds on a plate. Remove beef from marinade and press one side of each slice of beef into sesame seeds.
6. Grill the beef slices on an oiled grill or grill pan, sesame side up, for 1 1/2 minutes. Flip and cook the other side for 1 1/2 minutes until medium-rare. Do not overcook.
7. Slice beef into 1-inch (2 1/2 cm) strips. Place a halved pepper on top of each strip, sprinkle with crushed Pocky, and roll up. Thread onto skewers.
8. Arrange skewers on a serving platter and serve warm.

PIGGIES IN A BLANKET STUFFED WITH MAC & CHEESE

SERVES 12

Classic piggies in a blanket get a rock-star encore with the addition of smoky mac and cheese rolled right inside the pastry. The result is gooey, golden, and totally over the top. Perfect for parties, game nights, or backstage snacks, these bites are playful and indulgent.

INGREDIENTS

2 boxes macaroni and cheese

2 1/2 tablespoons spicy brown mustard

1 teaspoon smoked paprika

8 tubes of crescent pastry dough

1 28- ounce (790 grams) package little smokies (about 60 sausages)

3 tablespoons Italian dressing

3 teaspoons extra hot horseradish

INSTRUCTIONS

1. Preheat oven to 375°F (191°C). Line 3 baking sheets with parchment paper.
2. Prepare the macaroni and cheese according to box directions. Stir in 1 tablespoon spicy brown mustard and smoked paprika while mixing in the cheese sauce.
3. Unroll crescent dough and separate into triangles.
4. Place 1 little smokie and 1 tablespoon of mac and cheese on the wide end of each dough triangle. Roll up firmly, tucking in the sides, and add an additional 2 teaspoons of mac and cheese about an inch (2 1/2 cm) from the top and finish rolling. Leave a few noodles visible at the top for a playful, golden finish.
5. Place rolls seam side down on the prepared baking sheets (20 rolls per sheet), spacing about an inch (2 1/2 cm) apart.
6. Bake for 10–12 minutes, until golden brown.
7. Combine Italian dressing, remaining spicy brown mustard, and horseradish in a small bowl to make dipping sauce.
8. Serve rolls warm, drizzled with sauce or with sauce on the side for dipping.

These make me very happy. It's another combo of a special after-school food that my grandmother used to make me when I was a kid: mac and cheese and hotdogs on white bread. Combining all these into one pastry is just full of joy.

CHEEZY CHICKEN NUGGETS

SERVES 6

These nuggets are crunchy, tangy, and addictive, thanks to a dill pickle brine and a coating of crushed cheddar crackers. Air fried until crisp, they're paired with gooey cheese dip and pickle garnish. A childhood classic reimagined with bold flavors.

INGREDIENTS

1 pound 4 ounces (566 grams) chicken tenders

2 cups dill pickle juice

Nonstick cooking spray

1 box cheddar snack crackers

2 eggs

1 cup smooth-melting cheese

1/2 teaspoon black sesame seeds

3 dill pickles, cut into 1 1/2-inch (about 4 cm) spears, for garnish

INSTRUCTIONS

1. Cut chicken tenders into 1 1/2-inch (about 4 cm) pieces. Transfer chicken to a bowl and add the pickle juice. Refrigerate 1–2 hours.
2. Preheat air fryer to 400°F (204°C).
3. Apply a thin layer of cooking spray to the air fryer basket.
4. Crush cheddar crackers in a food processor or in a sealed bag with a rolling pin, until finely ground; transfer to a shallow dish.
5. Beat eggs in another shallow dish.
6. Remove chicken from brine and pat dry. Dip each piece of chicken into the beaten egg, then roll in cracker crumbs until coated. Repeat if needed for full coverage.
7. Arrange nuggets in a single layer in the air fryer basket. Lightly spray with cooking spray.
8. Air fry for 10 minutes. Flip the nuggets, spray lightly again, and cook for another 7 minutes until golden and cooked through.
9. While nuggets cook, melt cheese in a small saucepan over low heat. Stir constantly until smooth. Pour into a small bowl and sprinkle with black sesame seeds.
10. Serve nuggets hot with cheese dip and dill pickle spears on the side.

Cheez-Its® are my ride-or-die snack, from backseat bites as a kid to late-night road fuel as an adult. Smash 'em into a chicken crust, smother with Velveeta®, and boom: old-school, melty bliss.

LEBANESE CINNAMON CHICKEN SALAD

SERVES 6

Tiffany's heritage in a salad bowl! Warm, spiced chicken over crisp romaine with olives, parsley, and lemon. When you're not in the mood for salad, this baked chicken is equally tasty with rice and veg.

INGREDIENTS

Cinnamon chicken:

1 large whole chicken, cut into pieces

1/4 cup olive oil, any quality

1/2 teaspoon salt

1/2 teaspoon ground black pepper

1/4 cup chopped fresh garlic

1/2 cup fresh lemon juice

1/3 cup sliced Kalamata olives

2 medium onions, chopped

1 teaspoon ground cinnamon

1 teaspoon paprika

1 teaspoon cayenne pepper

1 teaspoon cumin seeds

Dressing:

1/4 cup first-press, cold-pressed extra virgin olive oil (pure and full-bodied)

1/2 cup freshly squeezed lemon juice

1 tablespoon coarse salt

1 tablespoon reserved pan juices

Salad:

1 large head romaine lettuce, chopped

1 15.5-ounce can (roughly 430 grams or 1 3/4 cups) garbanzo beans, drained

1/4 cup cherry tomatoes (approximately 8 tomatoes)

2/3 cup coarsely chopped parsley

INSTRUCTIONS

1. Preheat oven to 425°F (218°C). Place chicken pieces in a large casserole dish.
2. In a bowl, whisk olive oil, salt, pepper, garlic, lemon juice, olives, onions, cinnamon, paprika, cayenne, and cumin seeds. Pour marinade over the chicken.
3. Cover the casserole dish with foil and bake for 45 minutes. Remove foil, lower oven to 375°F (191°C), and bake 15 minutes more, until golden brown and fully cooked.
4. Remove cooked olives, set aside. Let chicken cool slightly. Shred 1 1/2 cups chicken into chunky bite-sized pieces. Reserve 1 tablespoon of the pan juices.
5. In a bowl, combine extra virgin olive oil, lemon juice, coarse salt, and reserved pan juices.
6. Add lettuce, garbanzo beans, cherry tomatoes, and parsley to a large bowl. Drizzle with dressing and toss gently to coat.
7. Top the salad with shredded chicken and olives. Drizzle with olive oil, a squeeze of lemon, and a pinch of salt, if desired.
8. Serve warm or at room temperature.

Cinnamon in savory dishes was something I first tasted at home, and it always reminds me of family. This salad version feels lighter but still deeply comforting. It's the kind of familiar, flavorful, and grounding dish I'd make after coming off tour that brings together old flavors in a fresh way.

Tamales aren't for everyone. A lot of folks in my crew just
don't vibe with masa. So, I flipped it: real deal marinated beef,
laid out on a pizza crust, with crispy fried masa sprinkled on
top for that special crunch. My family may not love tamales,
but in pizza form? They devour it.

TAMALE PIZZA

SERVES 6 (12 PIZZAS)

This mash-up brings together the deep, savory flavor of tamales with the fun, shareable spirit of pizza. Masa, shredded brisket, and fresh toppings combine for something hearty and playful. Your secret weapon here? Caldo de Tomate, a tomato-chicken bouillon you'll find in the Latin American section of any grocery store.

INGREDIENTS

Marinated brisket:

4 bay leaves

1/2 teaspoon garlic salt

1 teaspoon salt

1 teaspoon dried oregano

1 10-ounce (roughly 1 1/4 cups) can red enchilada sauce

1/2 cup water

1 medium beef brisket (6–8 pounds or 2720–3628 grams)

9 whole peeled garlic cloves

1 tablespoon Caldo de Tomate

1 Roma tomato, quartered

1 medium yellow onion, sliced thickly

1 jalapeño, chopped roughly

Masa and masa tortilla chips:

2 cups dry masa

1 1/2 cups water

1/2 teaspoon taco seasoning

1/2 teaspoon Cajun/Creole seasoning (salt-free)

1/2 teaspoon garlic powder

1/2 teaspoon chili powder

2 to 4 cups vegetable oil

Pizza crust:

2 13.8-ounce (roughly 390 grams) packages refrigerated pizza dough

1/4 cup olive oil

4-inch (10 cm) round cookie cutter

Additional toppings:

1/2 cup Cotija cheese, crumbled

1/4 cup thinly sliced green onions

1/4 cup diced black olives

1/2 cup salsa

1/4 cup fresh cilantro, chopped

INSTRUCTIONS

Marinated brisket:

1. In a large bowl, combine bay leaves, garlic salt, salt, dried oregano, red enchilada sauce, and water. Place the brisket in the marinade and refrigerate at least 8 hours, or overnight.
2. Preheat oven to 250–275°F (120–135°C). Place brisket and marinade in a deep roasting pan or Dutch oven. Add garlic, Caldo de Tomate, tomato, onion, and jalapeño, then cover tightly to seal in moisture.
3. Braise, covered, for 3–4 hours until fork-tender. Check every 45–60 minutes and add 1/2–1 cup hot water as needed to maintain moisture.
4. Remove brisket and rest 20–30 minutes. Shred finely and return to the liquid. Cover and braise another 20–30 minutes to blend flavors.
5. Taste and adjust seasoning. The beef should be juicy, tender, and ready for your pizzas.

Masa and masa tortilla chips:

1. In a large bowl, combine masa, water, taco seasoning, Cajun/Creole seasoning, garlic powder, and chili powder. Knead with your hands until a soft and slightly sticky dough forms. Reserve 1/2 cup of the prepared masa.
2. Divide reserved masa into small balls and press into thin tortillas. Cut into quarters. Heat the vegetable oil in a deep pot to 350°F (177°C) and fry the masa until golden and crisp. Drain on paper towels. Cut the chips into small pieces and set aside.

Prepare the pizza crust:

1. Preheat oven to 425°F (218°C) and line two baking sheets with parchment paper. Roll out pizza dough to 1/4-inch (roughly 0.5 cm) thick. Cut pizza dough into 4-inch (10 cm) rounds and transfer them to the baking sheets.
2. Brush the rounds with olive oil.
3. Spread a thin layer of prepared masa on each round. Bake 9–13 minutes, until golden.

To serve:

1. Top baked pizza rounds with shredded beef.
2. Add Cotija cheese, green onions, olives, salsa, cilantro, and masa chips.

My grandma Mimi was pure magic in the kitchen, and her German chocolate cake made every holiday feel legendary. I turned that memory into mini muffins, topping them with old-school Duncan-Hines or Betty Crocker frosting, just the way she'd do. Mimi gave me the freedom to play on her stage, the kitchen. That's why I'm rocking the kitchen these days too, in her memory. She'd be so proud. Love you, Mimi.

MIMI'S MINI GERMAN CHOCOLATE MUFFINS

SERVES 16
YIELDS 32 MUFFINS

German chocolate cake was my first choice for every birthday, but making an entire cake every time I crave these flavors is detrimental to the waistline. These rich, chocolaty mini muffins, topped with coconut-pecan frosting, pecans and coconut, are just the thing to scratch that sugar itch. Festive and perfect for parties, they're a nod to tradition with a modern, playful twist.

INGREDIENTS

Cake:

1/4 cup plain yogurt

1/4 cup milk

Nonstick cooking spray

3/4 cup all-purpose flour + 1 cup for coating muffin pan

1/2 cup unsweetened cocoa powder

1/2 teaspoon baking soda

1/4 teaspoon salt

1/3 cup vegetable oil

1/3 cup unsweetened applesauce

2/3 cup packed brown sugar

1 large egg, beaten

1 teaspoon vanilla extract

1 3/4 cup finely chopped roasted pecans.

3 tablespoons finely chopped unsweetened coconut chips

Frosting:

15 ounces (1 container or 453 grams) coconut pecan frosting

1 1/2 cups finely chopped unsweetened coconut flakes

32 pecan halves

32 unsweetened coconut chips

INSTRUCTIONS

1. Preheat oven to 350°F (177°C).
2. Spread whole pecans in a single layer on a baking sheet and roast 6–8 minutes, stirring halfway, until fragrant and golden. Cool completely, then set aside 32 perfect halves for topping.
3. In a small bowl, whisk plain yogurt and milk together and let come to room temp before adding to your batter.
4. In a medium bowl, combine 3/4 cup flour, cocoa powder, baking soda, and salt.
5. In a large bowl, combine vegetable oil, applesauce, brown sugar, room temp yogurt-milk mixture, egg, and vanilla. Once combined, slowly drizzle in 1/4 cup hot water and stir to combine.
6. Add dry ingredients into wet and gently fold, until the batter is just combined.
7. Add 1/4 cup finely roasted pecans and chopped unsweetened coconut chips; gently stir to combine.
8. Lightly spray a mini muffin pan with cooking spray, then dust with flour to coat. Spoon batter into muffin cups, filling about 3/4 full. Bake 12–14 minutes until a toothpick inserted in the center comes out with moist crumbs.
9. Cool muffins completely, in the pan, on a wire rack.
10. Unmold the muffins from the pan. Frost sides and tops with coconut pecan frosting.
11. In a shallow dish, combine coconut flakes and 1 1/2 cups chopped roasted pecans.
12. Roll the edges of each mini muffin in the chopped pecans and coconut.
13. Top each mini muffin with a roasted pecan half and a coconut chip.

SPINACH PIES

SERVES 8

Spinach pies are one of those recipes that feel timeless: warm, savory pockets that travel just as well to a party platter as they do to a casual weeknight table. The za'atar, lemon, and tender spinach filling is intoxicatingly fragrant, wrapped in golden, flaky pastry. Irresistible. They're simple to assemble but look like something you picked up from a bakery case.

INGREDIENTS

1 bag frozen puff pastry blocks (12 blocks/squares), 5 × 5 inches (roughly 12 1/2 × 12 1/2 cm), OR

2 sheets frozen puff pastry, thawed

1 teaspoon butter

1/2 of a medium white onion, chopped

18 ounces (510 grams) fresh spinach

2 cloves garlic, blanched and chopped

1 teaspoon salt

3 ounces (3/8 cup) fresh lemon juice

1 tablespoon za'atar seasoning blend

1 1/4 teaspoons white sesame seeds

1 teaspoon paprika

1/2 teaspoon dried coriander

1/4 teaspoon white pepper

Nonstick spray

1 egg, beaten (egg wash)

INSTRUCTIONS

1. Preheat oven to 375°F (190°C).
2. Thaw pastry in the refrigerator, ideally overnight.
3. Keep puff pastry in block form (do not roll out). Or if using pastry sheets, spread a little flour on a clean surface and slightly roll the thawed pastry sheet to make it 10 × 10 inches (roughly 25 × 25 cm) and cut into four 5 × 5-inch (roughly 12 × 12 cm) squares. Repeat for the other sheet and set squares aside in the fridge.
4. In a large pan, melt butter over medium heat. Sauté the onion until lightly browned, 5–7 minutes. Transfer sauteed onions to a bowl; set aside to cool.
5. In the same pan, combine spinach, garlic, salt, and a tablespoon of water. Cover and steam until wilted, 2–3 minutes. Drain excess water and set aside to cool.
6. In a medium bowl, combine spinach, onions, 1/3 cup lemon juice, za'atar, sesame seeds, paprika, coriander, and white pepper. Mix well.
7. Apply a thin layer of cooking spray to two baking sheets. Place 8 puff pastry squares on each baking sheet. Brush the edges with a light layer of egg wash.
8. Add one tablespoon of spinach mixture to each square. Gather the pastry edges, pinch them together in the center to seal, and brush with remaining egg wash.
9. Bake for 15–20 minutes. Bake until golden.
10. Lightly baste pies with the remaining lemon juice. Cool on a wire rack for 10 minutes.
11. Serve warm.

I love these little pies because they remind me of road snacks from my travels, something you can hold in one hand while you chat or listen to music. They're hearty without being heavy, and the za'atar gives them that herby punch I grew up with. They also reheat beautifully, which means I can sneak one the next day with my coffee and feel like I'm back on tour again.

VIP Meet & Greet

- BEEF WELLINGTON BITES
- SHRIMP WITH CILANTRO CREMA
- GLAM ROCK VEGGIE CHARCUTERIE SKEWERS WITH HARISSA DIPPING SAUCE
- NUOVO BLTS
- EGG ROLL CUPS
- CHEESE BALL TRIO
- PRETZEL CRUNCH WITH CHAI SPICE
- CITRUS HEAT CASHEWS
- ON THE GO LENTIL SALAD
- FARRO AND ARUGULA WITH BAKED PEACHES
- SLAW AND ORDER

On tour, food starts with a rider. A rider is part of a band's contract that outlines the food and beverages they are provided at a venue to ensure that the band and crew are well-fed and hydrated before, during, and after a show.

Performers can get very creative with their riders. You may have heard about Van Halen's legendary rider in 1982, which famously required a bowl of M&Ms backstage, with all the brown ones removed. The rider stipulated that if any brown M&Ms were found in the bowl, the band could cancel the show at full pay. But this wasn't an unreasonable rock star maneuver; it was a compliance test. To ensure the promoter had read their full 50-page technical rider, they buried "M&Ms (WARNING: ABSOLUTELY NO BROWN ONES)" deep within to ensure their technical specs were followed to a tee, which would produce not only a killer show, but help to ensure everyone's safety.

I've always tried to keep my riders fairly simple, with teas, coffee, deli meats, cheese, and items every venue can generally accommodate no matter where we are in the world. The reality is there's always more than the band can finish, and I hate to waste food. I used to take it back on the bus, but now I pull a portion aside, zhuzh it up, and bring it into the meet-and-greet before every show.

At my meet-and-greets, I've always been known for feeding people.

That platter—charcuterie, cheese, crackers, maybe a few beers—becomes part of the moment. Guests are surprised when I hand them something to eat, but that's the point. It makes the night personal for them and something that I hope means a little more than a basic, overpriced backstage experience.

People often say, "You're actually feeding me? We're sitting here with a cup of coffee, or wine, and talking?" Yes. That's the part I love. Food disarms people. It opens conversation. I'll hand you a cracker and say, "Try this cheese, add some greens, top it with sauce." And yes, I even carried condiments and a wide variety of hot sauces in my tour travel bag, because I take the art of a good bite that seriously!

That's not the norm; most celebrities don't sit down with you for twenty minutes, pour coffee or wine, and ask what's going on in your life. But that's exactly what I do. I like to hear people's stories and make it personal. I appreciate everyone who's been with me all these years, supporting new music, reminiscing about "I Think We're Alone Now" or "Could've Been," or just being kids of the 80s together.

I've learned fans don't just want music, they want connection. They want to see how I live, what I eat, how I share. A meet and greet is where the walls come down. Food makes that easy. You don't need tuxedos or champagne. You just need a plate, a bite, and a conversation that lingers.

The recipes in this chapter come from that energy. They're memorable, whether you're in a greenroom with paper plates or hosting friends with stemware. Each one sparks conversation, looks beautiful, and delivers a surprise in the first bite.

I love Beef Wellington Bites because they turn something grand into playful elegance. Puff pastry, tender beef, mushroom duxelles—they're approachable but still glamorous. Shrimp with Cilantro Crema is citrusy, never heavy, perfect before a long show; goodbye diner shrimp with red cocktail sauce! Glam Rock Veggie Charcuterie Skewers with Harissa Sauce are smoky, spicy, and colorful, like edible fireworks. Basically, they're my rider on a stick and so easy to pull together when unexpected company arrives.

Nuovo BLTs are a nod to reinvention. Chef Alicia transforms the classic bacon, lettuce, and tomato sandwich into an elegant Italian-inspired appetizer with bacon, arugula, grape tomatoes, and mascarpone. They taste familiar but keep you on your toes.

Who didn't love Chinese takeout nights growing up? Our Egg Roll Cups pack all the flavor of fried egg rolls into crisp little shells with explosively delicious pork meatballs—light, crunchy, and satisfying—without slowing you down.

Chef Alicia's Cheese Ball Trio is unapologetically retro, which is why I love them. They recall 80s parties I wasn't old enough to attend but dreamed about: shag carpets, gold platters, and the cheese ball as centerpiece. Bite-sized, they're cheeky, fun, and relevant again.

There are two party snacks that are must-haves for Meet & Greets: Pretzel Crunch with Chai Spice and Citrus Heat Cashews. I typically do a lot of press mornings and afternoons on show days. That doesn't always leave a lot of time to plan ahead for Meet & Greets, which generally kick off as early as 6:00 pm at some venues. Since Chef Alicia taught me her syrup method, I can zhuzh up boring pretzels and almost any nut combo you can imagine in 20 minutes or less. The fans go wild for these and I just nod and smile. Chef Alicia always has my back.

Not everything has to be decadent. On the Go Lentil Salad is my wellness anchor, hearty, clean and full of protein. It proves "healthy" can be flavorful and satisfying.

Keeping with that vibe, Farro and Arugula with Baked Peaches balances nutty and sweet. Chef Alicia and I love farro. It's an ancient grain and something we reach for when we're hungry, but on our best behavior.

Rounding out the set, my Slaw and Order . . . the name always makes me laugh! In the outskirts of Nashville, my home of over 20 years, we love our slaw, so I am thrilled to share my favorite slaw recipe with you. Sometimes I make it for 1. Sometimes I make it for a crowd. But it's never far from my fork.

This chapter represents quick ideas I actually use on the road, and a preview of what you might find at a Tiff Takeover or a VIP Meet & Greet. To fans who stand in the rain, who DM recipes and jacket photos, who show up for charity mornings and late-night shows, you are the reason these pages exist. For me, VIP isn't velvet rope energy. It's an open door, a plate, and a hug.

When you step into these pages, think of it as pulling up a chair to my table as a VIP guest. There's a plate waiting. The food is simple but thoughtful, dressed up just enough to shine. The recipes aren't about perfection, they're about presence. They're about the kind of night that feels like a premiere, even when it's a Tuesday. That's what VIP really is: not a gate, but a gathering. Not a velvet rope, but a kitchen table with glitter scattered across it. A place where food is an icebreaker, a jacket is a story, and the memory is yours to carry home.

CHEF'S TIPS—VIP MEET & GREET

These dishes rely on balance and presentation. Each component should look refined, hold its shape, and taste vibrant, even at room temperature. Precision and temperature management are key.

1. MANAGE TEMPERATURE CAREFULLY

Applies to: Shrimp with Cilantro Crema, Farro and Arugula with Baked Peaches, On the Go Lentil Salad

Cool proteins and grains completely before dressing to prevent separation or wilting. Assemble chilled items just before service for the best texture.

2. PRESERVE FLAVOR IN SMALL BITES

Applies to: Beef Wellington Bites, Egg Roll Cups, Cheese Ball Trio

Reduce portion size without losing intensity by seasoning fillings slightly more assertively than usual. Taste each element on its own before combining. If the dish tastes flat, it probably needs a pinch of salt.

3. PROTECT TEXTURE

Applies to: Citrus Heat Cashews, Glam Rock Veggie Charcuterie Skewers

Toast or bake nuts just until fragrant, then cool completely before storing. For skewers, keep dry components separate from dips or sauces until serving to preserve crispness.

4. BALANCE FLAVOR PROFILES

Applies to: Chai Pretzel Crunch, Citrus Heat Cashews, Harissa Dipping Sauce

Adjust flavor with salt and acid before adding sweetness or spice. Gently warming spice blends in oil helps release their aroma and ensures an even, rounded flavor.

5. PRACTICE RESTRAINT IN PRESENTATION

Applies to: Veggie Skewers, Nuovo BLTs, Slaw and Order

Leave space on platters for contrast and easy serving. Garnish simply and consistently. A few herbs or a drizzle of dressing is often enough. As Coco Chanel advised, "Before you leave the house, look in the mirror and take one thing off." The same principle applies to plating; simplicity always reads as confidence.

BACKSTAGE TAKEAWAY

Attention to detail elevates simple ingredients. Control temperature, texture, and proportion, and every bite will feel deliberate and composed.

BEEF WELLINGTON BITES

SERVES 8
MAKES 36 PIECES

These Beef Wellington Bites shrink down the grandeur of a classic into a hand-held showpiece. Tender cubes of seared ribeye, prosciutto, mushroom duxelles, and buttery puff pastry. They're elegant enough for the spotlight, yet easy to grab between greetings. Think couture in appetizer form: precise, indulgent, and ready for their close-up.

INGREDIENTS

Beef:

12 ounces (340 grams) ribeye steak

1 teaspoon salt

1 teaspoon pepper

4 teaspoons olive oil

8 ounces (227 grams) mushrooms, finely chopped

4 tablespoons shallot, finely chopped

2 teaspoons fresh thyme leaves

2 cups mayonnaise

Peppercorn dijonnaise:

1 cup Dijon mustard

4 tablespoons cracked peppercorns

4 ounces (113 grams) prosciutto, sliced into 36 thin ribbons

Pastry:

4 standard sheets frozen puff pastry, 10 × 15 inches (roughly 25 1/2 × 38 cm) , thawed

2 eggs, beaten (for egg wash)

Garnish:

4 tablespoons parsley, chopped (for garnish)

INSTRUCTIONS

1. Preheat oven to 400°F (204°C).
2. Freeze ribeye 15–20 minutes to firm. Cut into 36 1-inch (2 1/2 cm) cubes; season with salt and pepper.
3. Heat a skillet over medium. (Note: a well-seasoned cast iron skillet is best. If using a nonstick pan, add a small amount of vegetable oil to the pan.)
4. Sear beef in batches until browned on the outside (about 3–4 minutes per batch). Allow a little bit of space in between each beef cube to ensure the best sear. Once cooked, transfer the seared beef to a plate to cool.
5. To the same pan, add olive oil, mushrooms, shallots, and thyme. Cook over medium-low heat, stirring, until most moisture evaporates, 12–15 minutes. Set aside to cool; this is your duxelles.
6. In a bowl whisk mayonnaise, Dijon mustard, and cracked peppercorns. Reserve 1 cup for dipping; fold the rest into the cooled duxelles. Gently coat ribeye cubes in the mixture.
7. Wrap each cube in a prosciutto ribbon.
8. Unfold puff pastry and cut each sheet into 9 equal squares (36 squares, total). Place a prosciutto-wrapped cube in the center of each square, fold corners up to seal, and place seam-side down on a baking sheet lined with parchment paper.
9. Brush the puff pastry with egg wash. Bake for about 20 minutes, until golden and crisp. Cool the Wellington Bites on the sheet pan for 5 minutes.
10. To plate, transfer to a platter, garnish with parsley, and serve with the reserved peppercorn dijonnaise.

Beef Wellington is pure 80s glam but shrink it down and you've got next-level party bites. These little showstoppers are what you roll out when the VIPs are in the room: luxe, golden, and impossible to resist. Chef Alicia turned me onto this classic and gave it her own spin, and now it's my backstage pass to impress.

SHRIMP WITH CILANTRO CREMA

SERVES 4

This isn't your average shrimp cocktail. Poached shrimp meet a cool, tangy cilantro crema and nestle into crisp lettuce cups or endive spears. It's light and modern, perfect for a room that's buzzing. A fast, elegant bite that tastes like fresh air.

INGREDIENTS

Cilantro crema:

3 teaspoons salt

1 cup Mexican crema

2 tablespoons mayonnaise

1/4 cup chopped, fresh cilantro

2 teaspoons lime zest

2 teaspoons lime juice

1 teaspoon finely minced garlic

Shrimp and for serving:

20 peeled and deveined shrimp

10 large lettuce leaves

1 teaspoon chili-lime seasoning

INSTRUCTIONS

1. Blend 1 teaspoon salt, crema, mayonnaise, cilantro, lime zest, lime juice, and garlic until smooth. Refrigerate until serving.
2. Place shrimp in a saucepan and cover by 1 inch (2 ½ cm) with cold water. Add remaining 2 teaspoons salt. Bring to a gentle simmer over medium-high heat and cook 8–10 minutes, stirring occasionally, until shrimp are pink and firm.
3. Drain shrimp and transfer them to an ice bath for 1–2 minutes to stop the cooking. Pat dry and chill until serving.
4. Arrange two shrimp on each lettuce leaf or endive spear. Spoon 1–2 tablespoons crema over each and sprinkle lightly with chili-lime seasoning.

Shrimp is always a family favorite, but this dish takes it center stage with cilantro crema and zesty chili-lime seasoning. We whipped it up in Nashville with Chef Alicia, and my crew couldn't stop sneaking bites before it ever hit the plate. Easy to make, packed with flavor, it's the kind of dish that disappears fast with no leftovers. But in case there are, chop up the extra shrimp, mix with left over cilantro crema, chopped cilantro, and diced celery for a killer shrimp salad!

GLAM ROCK VEGGIE CHARCUTERIE SKEWERS WITH HARISSA DIPPING SAUCE

SERVES 6

Charcuterie meets the runway: bold colors, big textures, and a smoky North African-inspired dip, courtesy of our Pop Princess! These skewers are a showstopper. Playful to assemble and stunning on a platter, they're an instant conversation starter.

INGREDIENTS

Harissa dipping sauce:

3 tablespoons harissa paste

3 teaspoons olive oil

1/4 cup lemon juice

1 teaspoon minced garlic

1/8 teaspoon smoked paprika

Salt to taste

Skewers:

12 slices prosciutto rolled to look like a flower

12 slices charcuterie meats (salami, soppressata, capicola, chorizo, ham)

24 1/2-inch cubes of cheese (roughly 1 cm; a combination of Parmesan, yellow cheddar, and Colby)

12 small mozzarella balls, drained and patted dry

24 baby heirloom tomatoes

Skewers (cont):

12 cornichons, drained and patted dry

12 pickled okra pods, halved, drained and patted dry

12 olives (green, black, kalamata or mixed), drained and patted dry

12 cloves pickled garlic, drained and patted dry

12 marinated artichoke hearts, drained and patted dry

12 pieces of radicchio lettuce, cut in half and folded or rolled to look like a flower

2 small English cucumbers, sliced

12 skewers, 12 inches (30 cm) long

For assembly and serving:

4 ounces (113 grams) baby arugula

1 teaspoon dried harissa, for garnish

INSTRUCTIONS

1. In a bowl, whisk together harissa paste, olive oil, lemon juice, and minced garlic. Add paprika and salt to taste. Mix until smooth. For a thicker texture, blend in a small food processor.
2. Roll the meats into bite-sized bundles to look like a flower.
3. Thread 10–13 items per skewer. Mix and match for variety. Example: Tomato + Parmesan + cucumber + olive + garlic + salami + okra + artichoke + mozzarella + radicchio
4. Repeat until ingredients are skewered.
5. Arrange skewers on a bed of fresh arugula with a small bowl of dipping sauce in the center, or on the side. Lightly sprinkle the skewers with dried harissa.

Charcuterie may be a backstage staple, but who wants everyone picking off the same platter? I leveled it up by stacking up the classics: cheese, meats, veggies, and even spicy okra or pickles. Put it all onto skewers for an easy grab-and-go. With harissa dipping sauce on the side, they're glam rock, germ-free, and perfect for walking around backstage with your own plate. No platter, no problem.

NUOVO BLTS

SERVES 6

My Italian love letter to the BLT. Mascarpone stands in for mayo, arugula brings peppery lift, bacon stays legit, and the whole bite feels crisp, creamy, and new. One-hand snacks with big flavor, perfect for a crowd that likes to mingle. Primo!

INGREDIENTS

1 teaspoon olive oil

1/2 teaspoon lemon juice

12 crostini premade; or slice baguette 1/2-inches (roughly 1 1/4 cm) thick, brush with olive oil, and bake at 400°F (204°C) for 8–10 minutes, until golden

6 teaspoons mascarpone

3 ounces (85 grams) baby arugula

6 slices cooked, crispy bacon, cut in fourths (24 pieces total)

6 grape tomatoes, halved

INSTRUCTIONS

1. In a small bowl, toss arugula with olive oil and lemon juice.
2. Spread about 1/2 teaspoon mascarpone on each crostino. Top with a small nest of dressed arugula.
3. Add 2 pieces of crispy bacon and a halved grape tomato on each crostino. Serve immediately.

Why settle for a plain old BLT when you can glam it up? These little bites stack crispy bacon, arugula, and cherry tomatoes on crostini for a BLT that goes from okay to 10. Perfect for a cocktail lunch, game night, or even a fun snack for the kids. From every day to totally elevated.

EGG ROLL CUPS

SERVES 8–10

The takeout favorite deconstructed and lightened up. Crisp wonton cups cradle a juicy pork meatball made with gingery cabbage and green onion. They're tidy, crunchy, and perfect for a tray that needs to travel the room.

INGREDIENTS

24 wonton wrappers

2 teaspoons vegetable oil

1 pound (453 grams) ground pork

1 tablespoon sesame oil

3 green onions, minced + more for garnish

1 cup shredded purple cabbage, minced + unminced extra for garnish

1 teaspoon minced ginger

1/2 teaspoon minced garlic

Sweet and sour sauce, for serving

INSTRUCTIONS

1. Preheat oven to 350°F (177°C).
2. Brush both sides of each wonton wrapper with vegetable oil and press into a mini muffin tin to form cups. Bake 8 minutes, until lightly golden; unmold the wonton cups and cool them on a wire rack for 5 minutes.
3. Increase oven temperature to 400°F (204°C).
4. In a bowl, combine pork, sesame oil, green onion, cabbage, ginger, and garlic. Mix gently and form 24 small meatballs (about 1/2 ounce or 14 grams each).
5. Place meatballs on a baking sheet lined with parchment paper, and bake 15–20 minutes, until cooked through—165°F (74°C) internal temperature.
6. To serve, arrange the wonton cups on a platter. Nestle one meatball in each cup and top each egg roll cup with a little sweet-and-sour sauce. Garnish with minced green onion and remaining shredded cabbage.

Chef Alicia brought this fun little dish into my life, and it's been a party favorite ever since. We served them at Tiff Takeovers with sweet and sour sauce on the side, but my personal preference is a to serve them with a Sriracha kick on the side. All the flavor of a Chinese meal in one crisp, bite-sized cup and Vegas party vibes in every bite.

My mom was queen of the cheese balls in the 80s. I was so addicted to them that it took all the willpower I had not to park myself next to the coffee table and smear gobs of cream cheesy goodness onto my buttery butterfly-shaped crackers. The only way I could think to improve them was to make individual portions in three different flavors. And guess what? I still plant myself in front of these suckers at parties!

CHEESE BALL TRIO

SERVES 8

A glam upgrade to the retro party classic, now in three bold flavors. Ranch & Bacon is nostalgic and crowd-pleasing, Spicy Chèvre & Pistachio brings heat and nutty vibes, and Bleu Cheese Date adds sweet-savory depth. Serve them with crackers, sliced cucumbers, or even on skewers so guests can grab and go. Set them out together, and let guests pick their fave. Making our moms proud!

INGREDIENTS

Classic Ranch & Bacon:

1 cup (225 grams) cream cheese, softened

1 cup shredded sharp cheddar

2 tablespoons ranch seasoning mix

1 teaspoon Worcestershire sauce

1/4 cup minced green onion

1/3 cup finely chopped crispy bacon (for coating)

1/4 cup finely chopped parsley (for coating)

Spicy Chèvre & Pistachio:

6 ounces (170 grams) goat cheese

1/4 cup (2 ounces or 56 grams) cream cheese

1 teaspoon harissa paste or Calabrian chili paste

1 tablespoon honey

2 teaspoons lemon zest

1/3 cup crushed roasted pistachios (for coating)

Bleu Cheese Date & Walnut:

3/4 cup (6 ounces or 170 grams) cream cheese

1/3 cup (2 ounces or 57 grams) bleu cheese, crumbled

2 tablespoons finely chopped dates

1 teaspoon balsamic vinegar

Pinch of cracked black pepper

1/3 cup finely chopped toasted walnuts (for coating)

INSTRUCTIONS

1. In three separate bowls, mix the ingredients for each flavor (reserve the coating ingredients separately in 3 small shallow bowls).
2. Chill the cheese mixtures 20–30 minutes until firm enough to scoop.
3. Using a small scoop or spoon, portion each flavor into 1-inch (2 1/2 cm) balls.
4. Roll the Classic Ranch & Bacon balls in the bacon-parsley mix, the Spicy Chèvre balls in crushed pistachios, and the Bleu Cheese balls in toasted walnuts.
5. Serve with buttery crackers, cucumber slices, or skewer one of each, so guests can sample them all.

PRETZEL CRUNCH WITH CHAI SPICE

SERVES 6

"Chai" means tea in Hindi. And "masala" means spice blend. The quintessential blend of warming spices—commonly cardamom, cinnamon, ginger, cloves, and black pepper—is commonly used to flavor Indian spiced tea, my favorite coffee house drink. But since I don't roll deep with a barista 24/7, I created this addictive sweet and salty snack that I can munch on any time.

INGREDIENTS

1/4 cup pure maple syrup

1 12-ounce bag (340 grams) mini pretzel balls (unsalted preferred)

2 tablespoons masala chai

INSTRUCTIONS

1. Preheat oven to 300°F (149°C). Line a baking sheet with parchment paper.
2. Warm maple syrup in a small pan over medium heat, until thin and starting to bubble.
3. Add pretzel balls, stirring to coat evenly. Heat 1–2 minutes until syrup is tacky but not fully reduced.
4. Transfer the pretzel balls and any remaining syrup to the prepared sheet pan. Spread the pretzel balls into a single layer. Bake for 4 minutes, toss, and bake another 4 minutes, until the syrup is mostly set and the pretzels are glossy.
5. Remove from the oven and immediately dust with the chai blend, tossing to coat all sides. Cool on the baking sheet for at least 5 minutes before serving.

Chef Alicia's chai spice blend makes this Pretzel Crunch a total party in your mouth, like an elevated Chex Mix you'll never find in a store. Perfect as an office snack, road-trip fuel, or a holiday crowd-pleaser that'll have everyone asking where you scored the recipe. Easy, unexpected, and foodie-approved. It's snacking, leveled up.

CITRUS HEAT CASHEWS

SERVES 12

According to Tiffany's band, these cashews are "a little dangerous!" You'll recognize this cooking method from Pretzel Crunch with Chai Spice, with agave syrup standing in for maple syrup. You can truly spice these cashews any way you'd like. As a bonus track, I've shared the recipe for my Citrus Heat spice blend, which is also killer on seafood and mixed into tuna fish.

INGREDIENTS

Cashews:

1 1/4 pounds (567 grams) roasted, unsalted cashews

1/4 cup agave syrup

DIY Citrus Heat spice blend:

2 tablespoons lemon pepper

1 tablespoon smoked paprika

1 teaspoon dried oregano

1/2 teaspoon garlic powder

1/2 teaspoon onion powder

1/2 teaspoon ground cumin

1/4 teaspoon chipotle chili powder

1/2 teaspoon kosher salt

1/2 teaspoon sugar

INSTRUCTIONS

1. Preheat oven to 300°F (149°C). Line a baking sheet with parchment paper.
2. Warm cashews and agave syrup in a nonstick pan over medium-low heat, stirring 2–3 minutes until syrup is tacky and clings to nuts.
3. Spread the syrupy cashews in a single layer on the sheet pan and bake 10–12 minutes, tossing halfway, until glaze is set and glossy.
4. Upon removing from the oven, immediately sprinkle with the Citrus Heat spice blend and toss gently to coat. Cool completely before serving.

I whip up these Citrus Heat Cashews and pack them for international flights. They're way better than the sad little nut packet on the plane. A daily travel snack with just the right kick of spice, they're so addictive you won't want to share their first-class flavor. No upgrade required.

ON THE GO LENTIL SALAD

SERVES 12

Tiffany's lentil salad is a lifesaver when the day doesn't stop moving. It's hearty enough to fill you up, light enough to feel fresh, and easy enough to throw together while you're juggling three other things. I love how the lentils carry the bold flavors of lemon and balsamic, while the rose petal garnish adds just the right touch of glam.

INGREDIENTS

3 cups dry lentils

1/4 cup lemon juice + 2 tablespoons

1/2 cup Italian parsley, chopped

1/3 cup green onions, sliced (green parts only)

1 cup English cucumber, chopped

1/2 cup cherry tomatoes, halved

2 tablespoons olive oil

2 cloves of garlic, blanched and chopped

3 tablespoons coarse salt

5 tablespoons balsamic vinegar of Modena (thick balsamic syrup)

1 tablespoon garlic powder

2 tablespoons edible dried rose petals, for garnish

INSTRUCTIONS

1. In a large pot, cover the lentils with 1 inch (2 1/2 cm) of water. Add the lemon juice and soak the lentils for 30 minutes.
2. Rinse and drain the soaked lentils. Place them in a medium pot with 3 1/2 cups water, ensuring they are fully covered. Simmer the lentils with the lid on for 15–20 minutes, until al dente.
3. Drain the lentils and rinse with cold water to stop the cooking process. Transfer to a serving bowl.
4. Add the parsley, green onions, cucumber, and cherry tomatoes.
5. In a small bowl, whisk together the olive oil, chopped garlic, salt, balsamic vinegar, garlic powder, and remaining 2 tablespoons of lemon juice.
6. Pour the dressing over the salad and mix well. Refrigerate for 30 minutes before serving.
7. To serve, garnish the salad with dried rose petals

This lentil salad is perfect for all you on-the-go types such as me. It brings many comforting memories as it was a staple my Sito made, and a must have at every family event. Not only is this one of my favs, it's also nutritious, healthy, and vegetarian-approved. It's a dish that disappears fast. My twist? Rose petals for color and a nod to Lebanese cooking – fresh, vibrant, unforgettable.

I fell in love with this salad because it looks like something you'd find at a fancy hotel brunch, but it's really just a handful of smart moves. The roasted peaches are everything. They taste like sunshine and the chips on top always make people smile. It's the kind of recipe that surprises you in the best way, like an encore you didn't see coming.

FARRO AND ARUGULA SALAD WITH BAKED PEACHES

SERVES 6

This salad is proof that simple ingredients can punch way above their weight. Peppery arugula and nutty farro lay the groundwork, roasted peaches bring sweetness, and that truffle-lime vinaigrette ties everything together with a little luxury. Top it off with truffle-kissed potato chips and suddenly you've got a dish that feels playfully elegant.

INGREDIENTS

Dressing:

2 tablespoons + 1 teaspoon olive oil

1 teaspoon white truffle oil + 5 to 6 drops, for the chips

1 tablespoon lime juice

1 teaspoon agave syrup

1/2 teaspoon Dijon mustard

Peaches and salad:

2 ripe peaches, halved and pitted

1 tablespoon balsamic glaze or reduction

1/4 cup crushed classic plain salted potato chips

4 cups baby arugula, roughly chopped

1 cup cooked farro, cooled

2 tablespoons shaved Manchego

INSTRUCTIONS

1. In a small bowl, combine 2 tablespoons olive oil, 1 teaspoon white truffle oil, lime juice, agave syrup, and Dijon mustard and whisk until smooth.
2. Preheat oven to 375°F (191°C). Place peaches cut-side up in an 8 × 8-inch (20 × 20 cm) baking dish. Brush the peaches on all sides with 1 teaspoon olive oil. Drizzle the oiled peaches with balsamic vinegar and roast for 20–25 minutes, until bubbling and golden at the edges. Cool slightly, then dice and/or thinly slice the peaches.
3. Just before serving, pour potato chips into a mixing bowl. Lightly drizzle the potato chips with the remaining truffle oil, to taste. Gently toss until evenly coated.
4. Toss arugula and farro with the dressing. To serve, place the salad in small cups or on a large platter and top with peaches. Garnish with the crushed truffled chips and shaved Manchego.

SLAW AND ORDER

SERVES 6

Crisp, colorful, and built for a crowd. This slaw mixes cabbage, carrots, raisins, pepitas, and green onion with a tangy celery-seed vinaigrette. It's the fresh note that keeps a table balanced.

INGREDIENTS

Celery-seed vinaigrette:

1/4 cup apple cider vinegar

2 tablespoons olive oil

1 teaspoon Dijon mustard

1 teaspoon minced garlic

1/4 teaspoon celery seed

1/4 teaspoon black pepper

Salt to taste

Coleslaw:

16-ounce (roughly 450 grams) mixed bag tri-color coleslaw

1/4 cup carrot, shredded

1/4 cup golden raisins (unsweetened)

1/4 cup toasted pepitas (pumpkin seeds)

2 green onions, sliced thinly

1/8 teaspoon salt

INSTRUCTIONS

1. In a small bowl, whisk vinegar, olive oil, Dijon mustard, garlic, celery seed, black pepper, and a pinch of salt until emulsified.
2. In a large bowl, combine the tri-color coleslaw, carrot, raisins, pepitas, green onions, and a pinch of salt.
3. Pour vinaigrette over slaw and toss to coat evenly.
4. Let sit for 10–15 minutes to meld. Toss again just before serving; garnish with extra pepitas, if desired.

Slaw and Order, my foodie spin on my favorite show. This coleslaw skips the heavy dairy and goes tangy, zesty, and totally customizable to your flavor palette. Pepitas bring an earthy crunch, and if you're like me, toss in golden raisins. Tiff's favorite plot twist on this coleslaw case.

Backstage for the Band

- PUFFY CHEESEBURGERS
- PATTY MELT EGG ROLLS
- SURF & TURF DEVILED EGGS
- SKINNY QUESO
- FISH AND CHIPS ON A STICK WITH MUSHY PEAS
- 7-LAYER COMBO PIZZA DIP WITH CROSTINI
- TOUR BUS TACOS
- CORN RIBS WITH CARROT FLAKES AND CILANTRO
- LEMON PEPPER SMASHED POTATOES
- ALL THIS THYME SAUSAGE ROLLS

There's always a hot meal provided for the band backstage, usually brought in from local restaurants. The venues run a quick check beforehand in case of allergies, so the spread is safe, if not always glamorous. Over the years, I've taken what we've been given on the road and worked with Chef Alicia to create recipes that feel more elevated but still carry the soul of those late-night grabs. Some of them have become go-tos I'd happily serve at a family table.

You'll meet the band's latest obsession right up top: Puffy Cheeseburgers. Chef Alicia loves her puff pastry because it's so versatile and widely available. When we're driving to the next show, I'll grab a couple boxes of frozen puff pastry. By the time we reach the next venue, it's thawed and ready to rock. The band loves Chef Alicia's classic cheeseburger version, but her method works for an infinite number of combinations. We've stuffed them pizza-style with sauce and mozzarella, taco-style with spiced meat and beans, cottage pie-style with a spoon of mash, and even day-old Sweet and Sour pork right out of the takeout container. The crew loves them because they're hand-held, hot, and fantastic. Crisp on the outside and all the right nostalgia inside.

If the Puffy Cheeseburgers are the opening band, Patty Melt Egg Rolls are the headliner. They roll all the diner notes—seasoned beef, a whisper of caraway, onions, and American cheese—into wrappers and air fried until crispified. You can use jarred onion jam, which we do in a pinch. But we prefer to make Chef Alicia's roasted onions when we have time; they're super caramelized and so easy to make during sound check. The band loves them because they deliver the best part of a patty melt—perfectly seasoned beef and sweet-savory onion—without the nap-inducing bread crash.

Surf & Turf Deviled Eggs are pure glam. And if I have given you the impression that the band doesn't care about glam, my deepest apologies. Just because the band and crew often crave and prefer casual, simple food, it by no means defines their preference! Just as I adore spoiling my fans, I love preparing Chef Alicia's over-the-top Surf & Turf Deviled Eggs for the guys when I have the time. On the road, this can be as simple as putting in a to-go order at the closest steakhouse for filet mignon and a side of poached jumbo shrimp, and a pit stop at the nearest market for hard boiled eggs and fresh chives.

When it comes to queso, the band prefers processed cheese. And while Chef Alicia and I love nothing more than microwaving that big orange block with diced tomatoes and green chiles until molten, we've since embraced Skinny Queso, which is a lighter, cottage cheese version, spiced with taco seasoning. There are quite a few light queso variations online, but ours is better! Chef Alicia adds a generous tablespoon of nutritional yeast, which adds a deep, savory, umami note that mimics a cheesy tang. It helps the sauce taste more "Velveeta-like." The band devours it.

If the venue has an air fryer (or we've lugged ours in), Fish and Chips on a Stick with Mushy Peas gets the spotlight. We dredge chunks of white fish in flour, egg, and a rubble of crushed crispy onions, then air fry until the coating goes craggy and golden. When I'm home in between shows, I prefer legit, deep-fried fish, which is the version we've included in this chapter. As for the "chips," I am an air fryer convert. Toss your potatoes in a light layer of olive oil, tumble them into the air fryer basket and 20 minutes later, you'd swear you were in London's East End. The band always laughs backstage when I have a mic in one hand and Fish and Chips Stick in the other. After four decades in the biz, you learn how to multitask!

When I'm home in Nashville, Friday night is Pizza Night. My brother-in-law, our resident Chief Marketing Officer and Photographer Extraordinaire, goes to great lengths to make the dough and prepare mouthwatering toppings every week. The life of a touring musician means that I often miss out on his creations, which is why Chef Alicia's 7-Layer Combo Pizza Dip is so comforting to me when I am on the road. It's everything you want from a late-night slice without the bulky pizza box: crumbled sausage, peppers, onions, chopped pepperoni, olives, red sauce, and a blanket of cheese, bubbling in a cast iron skillet, with a side of crostini. And trust me, you need the sturdiness of a well-baked crostini to stand up to this hearty dip. And plenty of grated Parm and crush red pepper flakes on the side, please.

Next, a band fave: Tour Bus Tacos. What *can't* go in a taco?! We basically take whatever food showed up that night—chicken, beans, lettuce, even corn chips—and roll it in a tortilla. There are always tortillas on the bus; and after a show, when hunger finally lands, those tacos feel like salvation. Veggie or not, spicy or mild, it doesn't matter. They're a ritual, a way to turn leftovers into laughter, and proof that food doesn't have to be fancy to be memorable.

I know you will love my Corn Ribs with Carrot Flakes and Cilantro. We halve and quarter ears of corn into ribs, fry until they curl, then toss in a Baja-leaning rub—dried carrot for sweetness, chili-lime seasoning, a little cilantro, salt, and a squeeze of lime—and finish with crunchy toasted kernels, a.k.a. Corn Nuts. They look like confetti in a bowl and vanish in a flash. They're the thing someone tries for the first time and then announces, mouth full, that it's their new favorite food. We nod. We already knew.

Side dishes get star billing in this chapter, too. Roasted potatoes are familiar and kid-friendly, but Chef Alicia upgraded them to first class with a bright, grown-up twist. Her Lemon Pepper Potatoes are parboiled, smashed onto a baking sheet with butter, Parmesan, and lemon pepper, and roasted until lacy and bronzed. Five minutes to cool (if we can stand to wait that long), then we lift them off the sheet onto a gigantic platter. The band has been known to sprinkle bacon bits on top. We don't judge.

And because late-night hunger must be satisfied, I'm ecstatic to introduce you to my All This Thyme Sausage Rolls. It's puff pastry to the rescue again, wrapped around herby pork with onion, fennel, sage, and thyme, and then baked to a glossy, mahogany roll of heaven. We make a quick gravy on the stove and whip up a pot of mashed potatoes, then plate it like a pub supper that found a spotlight. There's always a hush when the first plate lands. The first time I made them for Chef Alicia, she was eerily silent. That was a first! When she finally spoke and told me it was the best bite of the year, I knew I nailed it.

Backstage food doesn't need applause. It just needs to work. It has to fit into twenty-minute windows, honor different bodies, and still taste like a hug you can hold. That's why the band is obsessed with these bites. Sitting on road cases after a show, beverage of choice in one hand and a backstage bite in the other, we're taking a minute to exhale and just be grateful we delivered for the fans one more time. These are the moments I live for.

CHEF'S TIPS—BACKSTAGE FOR THE BAND

These recipes are hearty, portable, and often rich. The key is managing fat and temperature so each dish feels satisfying, yet light.

1. REDUCE EXCESS FAT IN FILLINGS

Applies to: Puffy Cheeseburgers, Patty Melt Egg Rolls, Sausage Rolls

Drain meat thoroughly and cool before wrapping or baking. This prevents leaks and maintains crisp pastry.

2. MODERATE HEAT FOR CHEESE-BASED DISHES

Applies to: 7-Layer Combo Pizza Dip, Skinny Queso, Tour Bus Tacos

Melt cheese gently over medium-low heat to avoid separation. Combine hot and cold components at the last minute to preserve consistency.

3. FRY IN CONTROLLED BATCHES

Applies to: Fish and Chips on a Stick with Mushy Peas

Keep oil temperature steady—around 350°F (175°C). Work in batches to avoid crowding. Drain on a wire rack to preserve crispness.

4. STRUCTURE THE BITE

Applies to: Surf & Turf Deviled Eggs, Tour Bus Tacos, Corn Ribs

Layer textures intentionally. Use crisp bases beneath soft components to ensure clean, stable bites. For example, spoon taco fillings over lightly toasted tortillas, or serve corn ribs beneath creamy sauces to hold structure.

5. BRIGHTEN WITH ACID

Applies to: Lemon Pepper Smashed Potatoes, Corn Ribs, Mushy Peas

A small amount of citrus or vinegar at the end balances richness and enhances flavor clarity.

BACKSTAGE TAKEAWAY

Prioritize structure and balance. Control fat, maintain temperature, and finish with acidity for dishes that stay satisfying without feeling heavy.

PUFFY CHEESEBURGERS

SERVES 4

The band and crew need bites that travel from tray to hand without skipping a beat. Puffy Cheeseburgers deliver—beef, special sauce, onion, pickle, melty cheese—tucked inside flaky, golden pastry. The method is the star, so the filling can riff any way you like. They're dramatic, tidy, and wildly satisfying, the kind of snack that makes the room cheer when the platter arrives.

INGREDIENTS

3 tablespoons all-purpose flour

1 sheet puff pastry, thawed

3/4 cup ground beef

1/4 cup Thousand Island dressing

1/4 cup minced white onion

3 slices of American cheese, cut into thirds (9 pieces, total)

9 dill pickle chips

1 egg, beaten

3 tablespoons sesame seeds

Shredded iceberg or romaine, mustard and ketchup, for garnish

INSTRUCTIONS

1. Preheat oven to 400°F (204°C). Line a baking sheet with parchment paper.
2. Dust a cutting board with flour and roll the puff pastry to a 9 × 9-inch (23 × 23 cm) square. Cut into 9 equal squares.
3. Mix ground beef with Thousand Island dressing.
4. Place a heaping tablespoon of beef mixture in the center of each pastry square. Top the beef with a pinch of minced onion, 1 piece of American cheese, and 1 pickle chip.
5. Brush a thin border of egg wash around the edges of each square. Bring all four corners up to meet in the center and pinch to seal, enclosing the filling.
6. Place on the prepared baking sheet, seam-side up.
7. Brush lightly with egg wash and sprinkle each with sesame seeds.
8. Bake 23–26 minutes, until the pastry is puffed and deep golden. Cool 5 minutes.
9. Serve over a bed of shredded iceberg with zigzags of mustard and ketchup.

Backstage with the band after a live show or during a laid-back movie night, who doesn't love a cheeseburger? These Puffy Cheeseburgers hit the sweet spot, with all the flavor and none of the carb overload, so no food coma here. Fun, light, and totally satisfying, a Tiff Takeover favorite and the ultimate crowd-pleaser on any stage.

PATTY MELT EGG ROLLS

SERVES 6

All the sizzle of a diner patty melt—beef, American cheese, caraway seeds, caramelized onions—wrapped and air-fried to a crisp. As much as I love my rye bread, I don't miss it here at all, because this egg roll version delivers everything I need, without the morning-after guilt.

INGREDIENTS

Egg rolls:

1 medium white onion, sliced thinly

1/4 cup olive oil

1 tablespoon balsamic vinegar

1/8 teaspoon sugar

1 1/2 teaspoons salt

1 1/2 teaspoons black pepper

18 ounces (510 grams) ground beef

3/4 teaspoon garlic powder

3/4 teaspoon onion powder

3/4 teaspoon caraway seeds

12 egg roll wrappers

12 slices American cheese, halves (24 slices, total)

For serving:

3/4 cup Thousand Island dressing

3 green onions, sliced thinly

INSTRUCTIONS

1. Preheat oven to 350°F (177°C).
2. In a medium bowl, toss the sliced onions with the olive oil, balsamic vinegar and sugar. Season 1/2 teaspoon salt and 1/2 teaspoon pepper. Distribute evenly on a sheet pan and bake, tossing halfway through, for 15–25 minutes. Transfer roasted onions to a bowl; set aside.
3. Preheat air fryer to 375°F (191°C).
4. Brown ground beef in a skillet over medium-high heat. Season with garlic powder, onion powder, and remaining salt and pepper. Drain excess fat.
5. Lightly crush caraway seeds using a flat-bottom glass or small sauté pan; stir into the beef. Cool slightly.
6. Place an egg roll wrapper on a clean, dry surface, like a diamond. Spoon 2 tablespoons of beef in the center. Top beef with 1 tablespoon of roasted onions and two slices of American cheese.
7. Fold bottom corner of the egg roll wrapper over filling and tuck in sides. Moisten top corner with a dab of water and roll up tightly to seal.
8. Repeat with remaining egg roll wrappers.
9. Use a pastry brush to lightly coat the rolls with remaining olive oil and arrange in air-fryer basket in a single layer. Air fry 8–10 minutes, turning halfway, until golden and crisp.
10. Rest 2 minutes. Slice on the bias and serve with Thousand Island and green onions.

My mom loved patty melts, and I'll never forget the smell of those grilled onions, pure childhood magic. These egg rolls take that classic flavor and make it easier, lighter, and carb-conscious. A fun, unexpected way to serve up a comfort food favorite, classic flavor, turned up to 11. Mic drop.

SURF & TURF DEVILED EGGS

MAKES 12 DEVILED EGGS

Deviled eggs, dressed in their VIP best. A silky yolk filling gets topped with shrimp, a bit of filet mignon, and a sprinkle of chives. A legendary steakhouse entrée meets an 80s potluck classic.

INGREDIENTS

6 large eggs, hard boiled and peeled

1/2 teaspoon Dijon mustard

1/2 teaspoon mayonnaise

1 teaspoon crème fraîche

1/4 teaspoon salt

2 teaspoons minced fresh chives, divided

6 cooked jumbo shrimp, halved lengthwise

2 ounces (56 grams) grilled filet mignon (medium rare), sliced into 12 even pieces

4 tablespoons (1 ounce or 27 grams) caviar, optional

INSTRUCTIONS

1. Halve eggs lengthwise and pop yolks into a bowl; set whites on a platter.
2. Mash yolks with Dijon mustard, mayonnaise, crème fraîche, salt, and 1 teaspoon chives until very smooth. Transfer to a piping or zip-top bag.
3. Pipe about 1 tablespoon filling into each egg white.
4. Top each with a halved shrimp, one piece of filet mignon, and a small dollop of caviar (if using). Sprinkle remaining chives over the top.

For all the deviled egg fans out there. When you can't decide what to make, these are the guaranteed crowd-pleasers: a luxury twist that takes deviled eggs from simple to rockstar status. Why settle for plain when you can serve up these rockin' bad boys?

SKINNY QUESO

SERVES 10

Silky, spiced, and surprisingly light, this queso leans on cottage cheese for body and blends well, thanks to nutritional yeast. It's generous without being heavy, which makes it a VIP for my favorite vocalist. I always add a few dashes of hot sauce for Tiffany . . . you know, because she's Tiffany!

INGREDIENTS

3 cups full-fat cottage cheese

1/4 cup taco seasoning

1 tablespoon nutritional yeast

2 1/4 cups shredded Mexican cheese blend

1/3 cup pico de gallo +
2 tablespoons for garnish

INSTRUCTIONS

1. In a large microwave-safe bowl, combine cottage cheese, taco seasoning and nutritional yeast.
2. Microwave 3–5 minutes total, stirring every 45–60 seconds, until hot and melted but not boiling. (Stovetop: warm gently over low heat, stirring often.)
3. While the mixture is still warm, blend with an immersion or countertop blender until perfectly smooth. If too thick, add a splash of milk and continue to blend, until smooth.
4. Add shredded cheese and 1/3 cup pico de gallo. Stir to combine. If the cheese doesn't completely melt into the mixture, microwave in 30-second increments, until melted.
5. Transfer to a serving and garnish with remaining 2 tablespoons of pico de gallo. Serve with tortilla chips.

This queso is creamy, melty, and great on just about anything, but especially with authentic tortilla chips. It's a nod and a wink to my East LA days, and I can smell that cheesy goodness a mile away. Bold, nostalgic, and totally scoopable.

FISH AND CHIPS ON A STICK WITH MUSHY PEAS

SERVES 10

British pub joy, built for one hand. Crispy fish and vinegar-kissed potatoes get skewered in alternating bites with a spoon of mushy peas in between. It's playful, portable, and perfect for a room that never sits still. This is Tiffany's playful twist on the classic British favorite, the ultimate pub snack on a stick!

INGREDIENTS

Potatoes (chips):

4 large potatoes, cut into 1 1/2-inch (about 4 cm) cubes

2 tablespoons olive oil

2 tablespoons salt

Pepper, to taste

1/4 cup malt vinegar

Fish:

4 thick white fish fillets (such as cod or haddock; about 2 pounds/907 grams; skin removed), cut into 1 1/2-inch (about 4 cm) cubes

1 cup buttermilk

2 cups plain fish fry mix (seafood mix)

1 cup all-purpose flour

1/2 cup cornstarch

1 teaspoon baking powder

1 teaspoon salt

1/2 cup crispy fried onions, ground finely or crushed

1 large egg, beaten

2 cups club soda, refrigerated

1 tablespoon garlic powder

10–13 cups canola or vegetable oil

Mushy peas:

Small can mushy peas

2 tablespoons corn starch

Salt and pepper, to taste

For assembly:

1/2 cup pickled red onions

10–12 skewers, about 8 inches (20 cm)

Flaky salt

Lemon wedges

Tartar sauce

Inspired by my family and friends in the UK, who've supported me all along, this dish is my nod to my second home. Fish and chips on a stick with mushy peas, with chips crisped up in the air fryer for a lighter, modern twist. A little piece of England wherever I go, comfort food with a passport.

INSTRUCTIONS

1. Rinse potatoes with cold water 3–4 times until water runs clear, to remove excess starch. Drain and pat dry.
2. Preheat air fryer to 400°F (204°C).
3. Place dried potatoes in a large bowl, drizzle with olive oil, salt, and pepper and toss well until every cube has a light sheen.
4. Arrange potatoes in a single layer in the air fryer basket, close together, but not touching, to ensure maximum crispiness. Cook in two batches if needed.
5. Air fry for 20 minutes, turning halfway, until golden and crispy. Set aside.
6. Just before skewering, toss air fried potatoes (chips) with malt vinegar and flaky salt, to taste.
7. In a large bowl, soak the cubes of fish in buttermilk. Cover and refrigerate 20–30 minutes.
8. To a medium bowl, add 1 1/2 cups dry fish fry mix; set aside.
9. In another medium bowl, whisk 1 cup all-purpose flour, cornstarch, baking powder, salt, and crushed fried onions, until well combined. Whisk in the beaten egg and the cold club soda until smooth. Lastly, add the garlic powder and remaining 1/2 cup fish fry mix; stir to combine. Refrigerate the batter until you're ready to fry the fish.
10. Pour oil into deep Dutch oven or heavy pot at least 3 inches (roughly 7 1/2 cm) deep. Heat to 375°F (190°C). Maintain temperature.
11. Drain the buttermilk from the fish. Dredge each fish cube in plain fish fry mix, ensuring full coverage and sit in mix for 5 minutes.
12. When ready to fry the fish, shake off any excess dry mix and dip each fish cube into the refrigerated batter, coating fully.
13. Fry a few cubes at a time in the hot oil for 3–4 minutes, until golden brown and crispy. Remove with slotted spoon; drain on wire rack. Ensure oil remains at 375°F (190°C), allowing it to come up to temperature in between batches, as needed.
14. Add mushy peas in saucepan over medium heat. Slowly add corn starch. Stir occasionally, until thickened to moldable consistency. Season with salt and pepper, to taste.
15. To assemble, alternate crispy fish and chips on the skewers, placing peas and pickled onions in-between. Fill the skewers making sure to leave 2 inches (5 cm) at the bottom. Repeat for remaining skewers.
16. Sprinkle chips with flaky salt. Garnish with lemon wedges and tartar sauce.

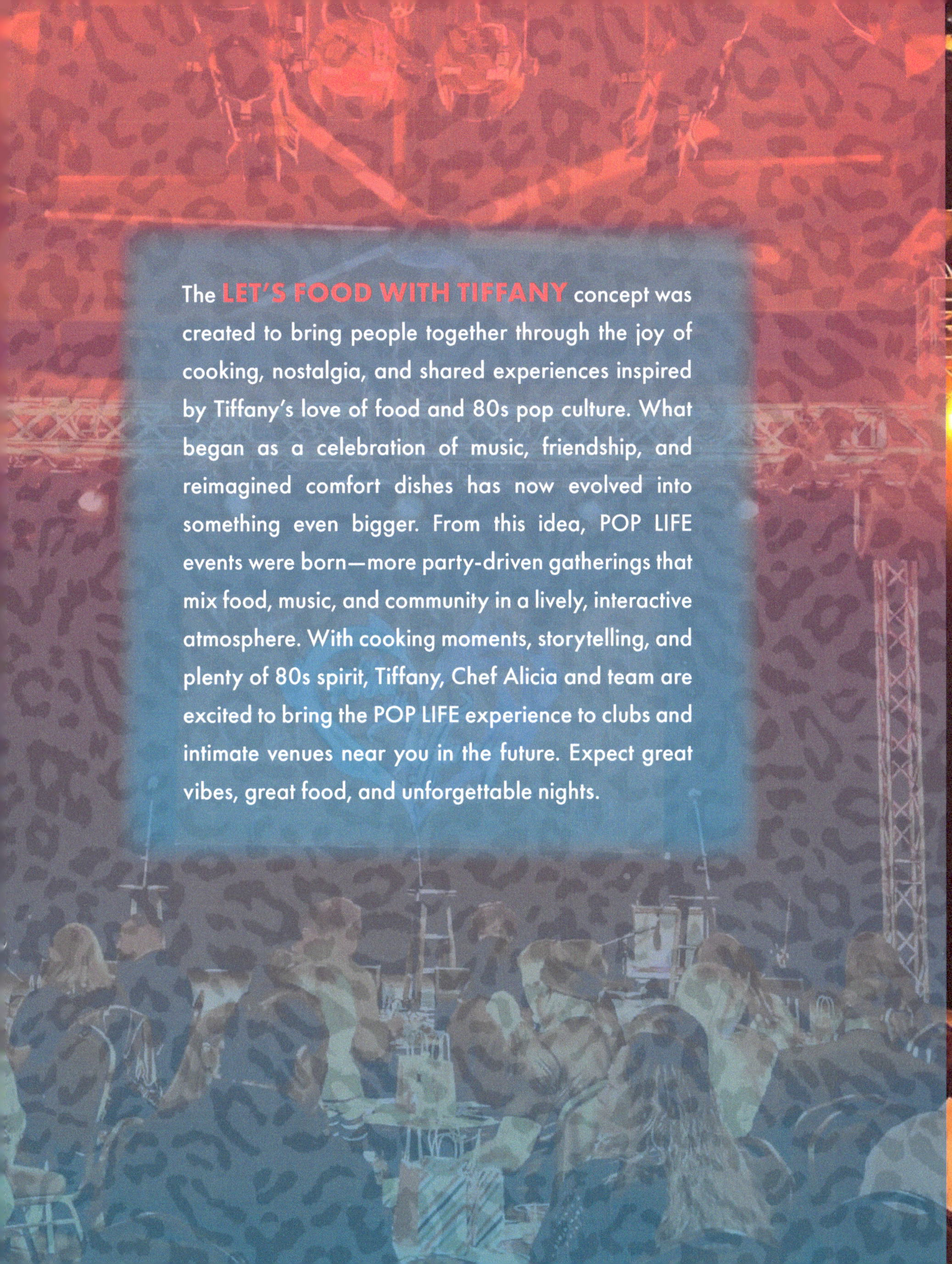

The **LET'S FOOD WITH TIFFANY** concept was created to bring people together through the joy of cooking, nostalgia, and shared experiences inspired by Tiffany's love of food and 80s pop culture. What began as a celebration of music, friendship, and reimagined comfort dishes has now evolved into something even bigger. From this idea, POP LIFE events were born—more party-driven gatherings that mix food, music, and community in a lively, interactive atmosphere. With cooking moments, storytelling, and plenty of 80s spirit, Tiffany, Chef Alicia and team are excited to bring the POP LIFE experience to clubs and intimate venues near you in the future. Expect great vibes, great food, and unforgettable nights.

7-LAYER COMBO PIZZA DIP WITH CROSTINI

SERVES 8

I love the original 7-Layer Dip in all its 80s glory. But when I *really* want to eat party food, I shove the storebought guac and canned refried beans to the side and whip out my cast iron skillet for this bad boy. Layers of sausage, peppers, onion, pepperoni, olives, sauce, and cheese bubble together into a mélange of molten combination pizza bliss. Pass the crostini, grated Parm, and crushed red pepper, and watch it disappear.

INGREDIENTS

8 ounces (226 grams) Italian sausage, cooked and crumbled

1 cup diced green bell pepper

1 cup diced onion

1 cup chopped pepperoni

1/2 cup sliced black olives

1 cup pizza sauce

1 cup (8 ounces or 225 grams) shredded mozzarella cheese

1 baguette, sliced thinly

3 tablespoons extra virgin olive oil

1 teaspoon salt

INSTRUCTIONS

1. Preheat oven to 350°F (177°C).
2. In a cast iron skillet, layer the following ingredients in order: sausage, bell pepper, onion, pepperoni, olives, pizza sauce, and mozzarella.
3. Bake 20–25 minutes, until the cheese is melted and bubbling. Cool on a wire rack while you prepare the crostini.
4. To prepare the crostini, heat oven to 400°F (204°C). Arrange baguette slices on two baking sheets lined with parchment paper; brush both sides of the slices with olive oil and sprinkle with salt. Bake 10–12 minutes, until golden.
5. Serve the dip in the warm skillet with crostini.

When you can't decide between dip and pizza, this 7-layer combo dip has your back. Gooey cheese, bold layers, and crispy crostini to scoop it all up. It's the go-to when the band can't agree on what they're most hungry for, with all the hits in one dish.

TOUR BUS TACOS

SERVES 4

Fast, flexible, and built for a crowd. Ground chicken or black beans get a quick spice bath, tortillas stay warm under a towel, and toppings stay simple. They're the foil-wrapped heroes of load-out: dinner you can actually eat in motion.

INGREDIENTS

Seasoned chicken or beans:

2 tablespoons olive oil or neutral oil

1 pound (453 grams) ground chicken or 1 14-ounce can (400 grams) of black beans, drained and rinsed

1 teaspoon chili powder

1 teaspoon smoked paprika

1/2 teaspoon garlic powder

1/2 teaspoon onion powder

1/4 teaspoon cayenne pepper

1/2 teaspoon salt

1/4 teaspoon black pepper

12 small flour or corn tortillas (street taco size)

Filling:

1 avocado, sliced or mashed

1/2 cup salsa or pico de gallo

1/3 cup crumbled Cotija cheese

Optional toppings:

1/2 cup shredded cheddar or Pepper Jack cheese

1 cup shredded lettuce or cabbage

1/2 cup sour cream or Greek yogurt

INSTRUCTIONS

1. Heat oil in a skillet over medium heat. Add ground chicken (or black beans). If using chicken, cook 6–8 minutes, breaking into small pieces, until browned. If using beans, warm 2 minutes.
2. Stir in chili powder, smoked paprika, garlic powder, onion powder, cayenne, salt, and black pepper. Add a splash of water (about 2 tablespoons) to make a light sauce; simmer 2 minutes.
3. Wrap tortillas in aluminum foil and heat for 5 minutes at 300°F (149°C), or toast directly on over a gas flame, 5–10 seconds per side.
4. Assemble tacos with 2–3 tablespoons filling, and the toppings of your choice.

Tour Bus Tacos are the ultimate fuel on the road: easy to throw together, totally customizable, and packed with flavor that travels well. I always keep spare tortillas on hand, and grabbing fresh ingredients from any local store means it's taco time anywhere. With my Let's Taco Taco Taco spice blend, you bring that East LA taste no matter where the tour bus takes you. It's taco time, anytime, any city; late-night jams after the encore.

CORN RIBS WITH CARROT FLAKES AND CILANTRO

SERVES 8

When the crew's hungry and the show is still hours away, these corn ribs are the backstage hero. A crispy, curly twist on classic corn, tossed in zippy Italian dressing and finished with a rock star rub of carrot and cilantro. They're crunchy, messy, and addictive in exactly the way good food should be.

INGREDIENTS

Spice rub:

1 tablespoon dehydrated carrots (dried carrot flakes), chopped finely

2 tablespoon dried cilantro

2 tablespoons fresh cilantro, chopped finely + extra for garnish

1 teaspoon garlic powder

Corn ribs:

4 ears fresh corn, husked

8 cups vegetable or neutral oil

1/2 cup Italian dressing

1/8 teaspoon flaky salt

INSTRUCTIONS

1. In a bowl combine dried carrot flakes, dried cilantro, garlic powder. Set aside.
2. Trim ends of each corn cob flat for easier handling. Halve crosswise, then lengthwise to cut each cob into quarters, cut each quarter in half again for eighths or "ribs" (use a sharp chef's knife and a steady grip).
3. In oil heated to ~175°F (79°C), fry ribs 2–3 minutes to soften. Increase oil temperature to 350°F (177°C) and fry ribs for an additional 3–4 minutes until curled and golden. Drain on paper towels and carefully transfer to a large bowl.
4. While hot, toss ribs with Italian dressing and dust with the spice rub and flaky salt. Garnish with fresh cilantro.

Corn ribs are made for the festival crowd. They're smoky, juicy, and perfect for eating with your hands while the bass drops. The cilantro brings the fresh high note, and suddenly this cheeky side dish takes center stage. With pure crowd-surfing flavor, they're street food with an attitude.

LEMON PEPPER SMASHED POTATOES

SERVES 4

Parboil, smash, and roast baby potatoes in buttery lemon-pepper-Parmesan until golden and delish. I can feed the entire band, and the crew, *and* the media with a few sheet pans of these babies. Even though these potatoes are inspired by my Distilled Spices Limoncello Pepper blend, basic grocery store lemon pepper is a more than suitable substitute, especially at midnight.

INGREDIENTS

8 ounces (about 6–7 potatoes or 226 grams) baby yellow potatoes

1 teaspoon salt

2 tablespoons melted butter

2 teaspoons lemon pepper

1/4 cup grated Parmesan cheese

INSTRUCTIONS

1. Preheat oven to 425°F (218°C). Line a baking sheet with parchment paper.
2. Cover potatoes with 1 inch (2 1/2 cm) of water. Season water with 1 teaspoon salt and bring to a boil over high heat.
3. Once boiling, reduce heat to medium high and simmer the potatoes until tender, 10–15 minutes. Pat potatoes dry.
4. Spread melted butter, lemon pepper, and Parmesan cheese on the sheet in an even layer.
5. Add potatoes and toss to coat. Use a flat-bottomed glass to press each to about 1/2-inch (roughly 1 1/4 cm) thick.
6. Bake 20–25 minutes until edges are crisp and Parmesan is golden. Cool 5 minutes and serve.

When we're in the studio laying down new tracks, these Lemon Pepper Smashed Potatoes are the comfort food that keeps us grounded. Crispy edges, fluffy centers, and that citrus kick bring just the right balance, keeping the mood level and the creativity flowing. Studio fuel with rock star flavor.

All This Thyme Sausage Rolls are my lyrical nod to my hit "All This Time," and to the family and friends I've made across the UK. Nothing says British comfort like a sausage roll, whether mini-sized for a quick bite or oversized to make it a meal. A classic that never goes out of style, this recipe is guaranteed to win over any Brit. It's definitely top of the pops. Don't forget the HP sauce!

ALL THIS THYME SAUSAGE ROLLS

SERVES 6

Want to see a pop star in her element? Watch Tiffany step off a London train, dash to a sausage roll vendor, and slip right back on the train with time to spare before the doors close. And her homemade, thyme-y version? It comes together nearly as quickly. It's generous, golden, and stops the band right in their tracks. I am completely hooked.

INGREDIENTS

Mashed potatoes:

3 pounds (1360 grams) russet or Yukon Gold potatoes

6 tablespoons unsalted butter, room temperature

1/4 cup whole milk, room temperature

Salt and pepper, to taste

Sausage rolls:

Nonstick cooking spray

1/4 cup finely diced red onion

24 ounces (680 grams) ground pork sausage

1/2 cup breadcrumbs

3 tablespoons English brown sauce + extra for drizzle

1 1/2 teaspoons salt

3/4 teaspoon ground black pepper

1 tablespoon garlic powder

1 1/2 teaspoons onion powder

2 tablespoons dried thyme

3/4 teaspoon fennel powder

1½ teaspoon dried rubbed sage

1/4 teaspoon paprika

2 sheets frozen puff pastry, thawed

1 egg, beaten (egg wash)

Flaky salt (optional)

Gravy:

4 teaspoons powdered beef gravy

1 1/4 cups cold water

2 tablespoons Worcestershire sauce

Garnish:

Fresh thyme

INSTRUCTIONS

1. Peel and cube potatoes (1 inch). Cover with cold salted water; boil, then simmer 15–20 minutes until tender. Drain; return to pot on low for 1 minute to evaporate moisture. Mash with butter and milk; season to taste. Keep warm.
2. Preheat oven to 400°F (204°C). Line a baking sheet with parchment paper.
3. Lightly sauté diced onion in cooking spray with a pinch of salt 3–4 minutes; cool.
4. In a bowl, combine cooled onion, sausage, breadcrumbs, English brown sauce, salt, black pepper, garlic powder, onion powder, dried thyme, fennel, sage, and paprika. Mix just to combine.
5. Dust a clean surface with flour. Stack the two pastry sheets and roll to 13 × 15 inches (roughly 33 × 38 cm) . Cut into three 5 × 13-inch (roughly 12 × 33 cm) strips.
6. Divide sausage filling into 3 equal logs and place down the length of each strip. Roll pastry to encase, sealing with beaten egg; crimp ends.
7. Place seam-side down on the baking sheet, brush tops with egg, sprinkle flaky salt if using, and cut 3 diagonal slits in each.
8. Bake 20–25 minutes until golden and the sausage reaches 160°F (71°C) internal.
9. In a small saucepan, whisk powdered gravy with a little of the cold water to make a paste, then whisk in remaining water. Bring to a boil, whisking, until thickened; stir in Worcestershire sauce.
10. Slice each roll into 3 pieces (9 total). Serve with the mashed potatoes and gravy. Garnish with fresh thyme and a drizzle of English brown sauce.

After Party

- CRAB-STUFFED CHERRY TOMATOES
- PULLED PORK CROSTINI WITH POMEGRANATE-CRUSH REDUCTION
- WALDORF CHICKEN SALAD
- TRASH CAESAR
- ANTIPASTO PASTA BAKE
- ROLLED MUSHROOM LASAGNA
- CHERRY COLA BROWNIES
- POPPING CANDY BARK
- MAPLE DONUT PUDDING
- THAI TURKEY SLIDERS
- MANGO GINGER CHUTNEY

After Party is when the real party begins! Some of my favorite shows come with after parties. We don't often get to do them, but when we do, we like to do them right. It's family in the room if they made the show, Team Tiff in the crowd, the band unwinding with a laugh, and fans who don't want the night to end. It feels less like an event and more like a celebration, the kind where the curtain has dropped but the joy keeps rolling. There's not always much time to prepare, but we make it count.

That's the heartbeat of After Party. These recipes are built for those moments when the music is over but the night isn't finished. They're elevated enough to feel like an encore, but flexible enough to pull off when you're tired, but buzzing and grateful.

Of course, no party would be complete without Chef Alicia's, or shall we say her mom Tina's, Crab-Stuffed Cherry Tomatoes. In the 80s, Chef Alicia's parents were infamous for hosting parties with some of America's most influential politicians, from a former U.S. Secretary of Defense and Director of the CIA, to senators, members of Congress, and visiting dignitaries. There were no slow cookers at her house. Hors d'oeuvres were expertly plated on sterling silver platters lined with doilies. Having spent time with Tina, there's no question that her gastronomic flair runs deep in Chef Alicia's veins, as does her love for fresh Dungeness crab, straight from the chilly waters of the Pacific Ocean.

By contrast, you will adore Pulled Pork Crostini with Pomegranate-Crush Reduction, an ode to Crush, my favorite childhood soda. That classic, citrusy fizz brings me back to the sound of a mall arcade on a Friday night, smiling when I think about the friends I knew I'd never lose. They fly off a platter because they deliver crunch, sweet, and salt in two bites. But don't stop at crostini! Use this pulled pork for BBQ sandwiches, saucy burritos, and crisped up on a Sunday morning with some fried eggs. Thank me later.

Salads have swagger at midnight. I am a sucker for loaded salads that are unapologetically bold and phenomenally delicious. Waldorf Chicken Salad brings crisp apples, celery, toasted nuts, and tender chicken into a bowl that feels both dressed-up and chilled down. A little sweet, a little crunch, not too creamy. For Caesar fans who grew up and got mischievous, Trash Caesar is our punk remix. Shatter-crunch croutons, shrimp, and a few unexpected pantry heroes make it hit louder than it looks. It's a salad you eat like popcorn. If you're into basic garden salad with bottled dressing, press FF on your cassette player. These tracks are anything but ordinary.

Many performers keep their after parties pretty light. That's not how I do things. If my band, friends, family, and fans want to hang out late, I need some dishes that will stick to their ribs. Antipasto Pasta Bake works every time because it's a total pantry pull. At any given time, we have a few bags of pasta shells on the bus, as well as salami, roasted red peppers and olives. A quick run to the store for artichoke hearts and some good Parmesan, and boom! Right in the oven. Rolled Mushroom Lasagna? Same vibe. I've even used canned mushrooms in a pinch. The key is good quality ricotta and a great jarred marina sauce. Once baked, the lasagna rolls are so elegant, your guests will think you've sprung for a fancy caterer.

I've always had a sweet tooth after I perform. And I absolutely know where it comes from. As a kid, I spent afternoons in my grandma's kitchen, singing to the tiles and playing dress-up with her scarves and jewelry. By the time my mom came to pick me up, I'd be in full costume, belting in front of the TV while my grandfather tried to watch the six o'clock news. Finally, he'd laugh and say, "Let's see what your Mimi has in the kitchen for you." Cookies, donuts, little bites to keep me occupied and quiet down the show. He was trying to save his news time, but he also gave me my first taste of post-performance indulgence. That ritual stuck. To this day, if I've given my all on stage, I crave something sweet to close the loop, a wink back to Mimi and Pa, and a nod to the kid who never stopped performing.

Cherry Cola Brownies scratches that itch for me every time. Dark, fudgy and jeweled with maraschino cherries, they cut into squares that leave a shiny crumb on the knife and a hush at the first bite. The sweet soda lifts the cocoa without making the brownies feel heavy, and the cherry sounds like the hook from a song you forgot you loved. We stack them on a cake stand and eat the corner pieces first; that's the law.

Chef Alicia's Popping Candy Bark is a straight-up knockout. And it's simple to prepare large batches very quickly, the hallmark of a killer After Party. And because the night belongs to sweet things that love the spotlight, Maple Donut Pudding shows up like the friend who walks in with a bouquet of flowers. An homage to my mom, I cut up day-old maple donuts, cover them in custard perfumed with orange zest, and bake until golden at the edges, but soft in the middle. Bread pudding, it's time to retire. We appreciate your service and we'll take it from here.

Rounding out the night, my Thai Turkey Sliders carry the room. Chili, herbs, a little citrus, a swipe of creamy heat, and soft buns toasted just enough. They are late-night diplomacy at its finest. And when you make these sliders, I insist that you also make their sidekick, Mango Ginger Chutney. Sunshine in a jar. Pure. And simple.

After Party is when we exhale. I will usually slip into something more comfortable, usually a Children Behave tee, and if it's cold, one of my custom Miracle Network motorcycle jackets. The band changes out of their denim and leather into sweatpants and hoodies. It's family in town, bandmates still buzzing, fans who linger a little longer because the night is too good to end. It's the kid in the kitchen who got sweets for singing and is all grown up and still celebrating. It's where memories, music, and food overlap in a way that feels almost ceremonial. Make a dessert. Make two. Put your feet on the coffee table and let your inner night owl have some fun. If you can still hear the fizz in the Crush can, the party isn't over.

CHEF'S TIPS—AFTER PARTY

These dishes are designed for relaxed entertaining: indulgent but manageable, and easy to serve once guests arrive. The key is to bring richness and freshness into harmony and organize your prep so each dish holds its texture and flavor from first bite to last.

1. KEEP EVERY BITE INTACT

Applies to: Crab-Stuffed Cherry Tomatoes, Pulled Pork Crostini, Thai Turkey Sliders

Handheld foods fall apart fast when overfilled or prepped too early. Keep components separate until service and apply sauces with a light touch to preserve crunch and color.

2. ADD CONTRAST TO SWEET DESSERTS

Applies to: Cherry Cola Brownies, Maple Donut Pudding, Popping Candy Bark

Rich desserts benefit from contrast. Add salt, citrus zest, or toasted nuts to prevent sweetness from overwhelming the palate. Bake just until set and allow desserts to rest before cutting for clean slices and even texture.

3. MANAGE PASTA AND BAKED LAYERS WITH PRECISION

Applies to: Rolled Mushroom Lasagna, Antipasto Pasta Bake

Avoid overcooking noodles; they will continue to soften in the oven. Bake until edges are lightly golden, then rest on the counter before slicing so layers hold together. A bit of extra sauce on the side keeps portions moist without oversaturating the pan.

4. DRESS SALADS JUST BEFORE SERVING

Applies to: Waldorf Chicken Salad, Trash Caesar

Dress only what will be served immediately. Keep extra dressing on the side to maintain texture and control moisture. For cold salads, chill components separately and combine shortly before plating.

5. REDUCE SAUCES WITH PATIENCE

Applies to: Mango Ginger Chutney, Pomegranate-Crush Reduction

Cook slowly over medium heat until thickened and glossy. Stir often and test by running a spoon through the mixture. It should be thick enough to leave a quick line before filling in. Proper reduction concentrates flavor without burning or caramelizing too far.

BACKSTAGE TAKEAWAY

Plan each dish to hold its quality over time. Work in stages, be aware of texture, and aim for contrast—richness complemented by freshness, and warmth supported by structure.

CRAB-STUFFED CHERRY TOMATOES

SERVES 8

Festive, bright, and party-ready, my mom's Crab-Stuffed Cherry Tomatoes is the only 80s recipe in this book that doesn't require a reboot. I now realize that my mom prepared at least a dozen more than she needed for parties, because I'd constantly "sneak" a few at a time when she wasn't watching. Spoiler alert: She was *always* watching!

INGREDIENTS

16 cherry tomatoes

3/4 cups (5 ounces or 141 grams) cream cheese, softened

1 teaspoon onion powder

3 tablespoons finely diced chives

2 teaspoons mayonnaise

2 teaspoons heavy cream

1 teaspoon hot sauce

5 ounces (141 grams) Dungeness crab, or best available crab

1 teaspoon paprika, for garnish

INSTRUCTIONS

1. Remove stems from tomatoes, if present.
2. Slice a thin layer off the bottom of the tomatoes and invert on a plate such that the stem side is now the base. Scoop out the seeds from the top side to form tomato cups.
3. In a bowl, mix cream cheese, onion powder, 2 tablespoons chives, mayonnaise, heavy cream, and hot sauce until smooth.
4. Gently fold in the crab.
5. Fill each tomato cup with about 1 teaspoon filling.
6. Garnish with remaining chives and a light sprinkle of paprika. Chill until serving.

When the party winds down but the cravings kick in, these Crab-Stuffed Cherry Tomatoes are the perfect bite. Chef Alicia first brought them into one of our Nashville recording sessions, and honestly, this recipe might have been a way bigger hit than the song we were cutting that day. Sweet, juicy tomatoes filled with rich, savory crab. They're light enough to keep the night rolling, but still a celebration in every bite. After party fuel, one perfect pop at a time, because the night doesn't end here.

PULLED PORK CROSTINI WITH POMEGRANATE-CRUSH REDUCTION

SERVES 12

Crunchy crostini, juicy pork, and a glossy citrus-pomegranate drizzle; two-bite fireworks. Another Tiffany chart topper! They're styled to perfection but come together with simple components you can make ahead. Perfect for passing around while the stories get good.

INGREDIENTS

Pulled pork:

2 pounds (207 grams) boneless pork shoulder

1 teaspoon coarse salt

1 teaspoon black pepper

1 tablespoon smoked paprika

1 teaspoon garlic powder

1 teaspoon ground cumin

1 cup chicken broth

1 tablespoon apple cider vinegar

Crostini:

1 baguette, sliced into 1/2-inch (roughly 1 1/4 cm) rounds (about 40 slices)

2 tablespoons olive oil

1 teaspoon salt

Pomegranate-Crush drizzle:

1/2 cup pomegranate juice

1/2 cup Crush orange-flavored soda

Fresh thyme leaves to garnish

INSTRUCTIONS

1. Preheat to 300°F (149°C). Rub pork with salt, black pepper, paprika, garlic powder, and cumin. Place in Dutch oven with broth and vinegar; cover and roast 3 1/2 hours, flipping once. Uncover and roast an additional 30 minutes to brown.
2. Once cooked, transfer the pork and cooking liquid to a large bowl; shred and cool.
3. Preheat oven to 400°F (204°C). Arrange the baguette slices on a baking sheet lined with parchment paper.
4. Brush the baguette slices with oil. Season each with a pinch of coarse salt and bake 8–10 minutes, flipping halfway, until golden.
5. In a small saucepan, combine pomegranate juice and orange Crush. Bring to a boil over high heat; reduce to medium low and simmer 10–15 minutes, stirring frequently, until syrupy. Cool the reduction for 5 minutes.
6. To assemble, drizzle each crostini with a little bit of the pomegranate-Crush reduction, and top with 1/4 teaspoon minced garlic, and 1 or 2 tablespoons of warm pulled pork. Drizzle the pork with the reduction. Garnish with fresh thyme leaves.

This pulled pork crostini is straight out of an 80s mixtape: bold, sweet, and a little unexpected with that pomegranate-orange Crush reduction. It's tangy, elevated, and dripping with nostalgia, because who doesn't want to feel forever young after the lights go down? An after-party bite with flavor that never skips a beat.

WALDORF CHICKEN SALAD

SERVES 4

You know you're Gen X when one of your recipes is featured in *AARP: The Magazine*. But, hey, I was in good company; Kevin Costner and his adorable yellow lab, Bobby, graced the cover! Forget the cloyingly sweet versions you may have tried at potlucks. This rendition is ready for prime time.

INGREDIENTS

1 1/2 teaspoons sugar

1 teaspoon lemon juice

1 teaspoon orange juice

1/4 cup mayonnaise

1 cup diced apple (about 1 medium apple)

2/3 cup diced celery

3/4 cup halved grapes

1/3 cup chopped walnuts

8 ounces (227 grams) cooked chicken breast, cubed

Butter lettuce or romaine lettuce spears, for serving

1 tablespoon orange zest

INSTRUCTIONS

1. In a large bowl, whisk sugar, lemon juice, orange juice, and mayonnaise until smooth.
2. Add apple, celery, grapes, walnuts, and chicken; toss gently to coat.
3. Serve chilled or at room temperature on lettuce spears. Garnish with orange zest.

I've always loved those posh Waldorf salads at places like the Langham in London or the Ritz in New York, total hotel royalty vibes. But this version isn't just for five-star lobbies; it's an after-party classic that brings the same elegance to your own table. With crisp apples, grapes, and chicken dressed to impress, it's five-star flavor without the check-in.

TRASH CAESAR

SERVES 4

Our Trash Caesar is my tribute to Garbage Caesar, the gloriously over-the-top Italian steakhouse salad Tiffany and I always order at Piero's in Las Vegas. That place is pure old-school glamour, famously cast as *The Leaning Tower* in *Casino*, where Nicky Santoro bragged about his milk-fed veal in the early 80s. It's the kind of restaurant where celebrities go to be seen, but never bothered.

INGREDIENTS

2 romaine hearts, chopped

4 hearts of palm spears, sliced

1 large avocado, diced

1 cup diced heirloom tomato

2 cups croutons

2 cups bay shrimp

2 cups grated Parmesan cheese, + more for garnish

1 teaspoon minced garlic

2 tablespoons lemon juice

2 teaspoons anchovy paste

1 teaspoon Dijon mustard

2 teaspoons Worcestershire sauce

4 tablespoons olive oil (or 1/4 cup)

2 tablespoons sour cream

1 teaspoon black pepper

INSTRUCTIONS

1. In a large bowl, combine romaine, hearts of palm, avocado, tomato, croutons, shrimp, and 1 cup Parmesan cheese.
2. In a small bowl, whisk remaining 1 cup Parmesan with garlic paste, lemon juice, anchovy paste, Dijon, Worcestershire, olive oil, sour cream, and black pepper until smooth.
3. Toss salad with dressing. Garnish with extra Parmesan and cracked pepper; serve immediately.

Trash Caesar is the salad built for the hair bands, all attitude, but still watching the waistlines after the show. Crunchy, tangy, and a little over the top, it's proof that even rockers need their greens. An after-party riff that keeps the flavor loud and the calories low.

ANTIPASTO PASTA BAKE

SERVES 8

Tiffany can feed a crowd with this one. It's our go-to way to turn leftover charcuterie and cheese into something worthy of an encore. On tour, she's known to scoop up odds and ends from specialty markets and artisan purveyors, then fold them into this rich, baked pasta. It's one of our favorite "double dip" recipes: Taleggio headlines a one-night-only Antipasto Bake in Illinois, then makes a comeback in Nashville for Pizza Night on Friday.

INGREDIENTS

1 pound (450 grams) small pasta shells (one full box)

2 cups heavy cream

12 ounces (340 grams) Taleggio cheese, cubed

4 tablespoons jarred roasted red pepper bruschetta

2 cups assorted deli meats (e.g., mortadella, salami, bresaola), diced

24 green olives, sliced

8 artichoke hearts, quartered

4 tablespoons grated Parmesan cheese

Cooking spray

INSTRUCTIONS

1. Preheat oven to 350°F (177°C). Coat a 9 × 13-inch (roughly 23 × 33 cm) baking dish with cooking spray.
2. Boil pasta in salted water until al dente; drain.
3. Heat cream over medium low; add Taleggio and roasted red pepper bruschetta. Stir until smooth.
4. In a large bowl, combine pasta, diced meats, olives, artichokes, and cream sauce; mix to coat.
5. Transfer to the baking dish and sprinkle with Parmesan. Bake 25 minutes until bubbling and lightly golden. Rest 5 minutes before serving.

Antipasto Pasta Bake is the dish that keeps the night alive; it's cheesy, hearty, and loaded with all the bold flavors you crave after the lights go down. It's Italian comfort with a rock 'n' roll edge, perfect after-hours cuisine. Make it your own by tossing in those lingering leftovers from the fridge, an encore dish that always brings the crowd back for more.

ROLLED MUSHROOM LASAGNA

SERVES 8

I certainly didn't invent rolled lasagna, but I would love to shake the hand of the person who did. It's the perfect assembly line recipe! Drummer is on noodles, keyboardist is on ricotta, lead guitarist is on sauteed mushrooms, and the back-up singers roll 'em up to bake. And talk about portion management: one roll per person. Make 2 or make 20. My kind of scales.

INGREDIENTS

8 dried lasagna sheets

1 cup whole milk ricotta

1/2 cup shredded mozzarella

1/2 cup grated Parmesan cheese

1 1/2 teaspoons onion powder

1 teaspoon garlic powder

1 teaspoon dried thyme

1/4 teaspoon salt

1/4 teaspoon black pepper

1/4 cup chopped fresh parsley

Nonstick cooking spray

1 cup jarred marinara

1 cup finely diced sautéed mushrooms (e.g., cremini or button)

Fresh basil, for garnish

INSTRUCTIONS

1. Preheat oven to 375°F (190°C).
2. Boil lasagna sheets 6–8 minutes in well-salted water until pliable but not fully cooked; drain and pat dry.
3. In a bowl, mix ricotta, mozzarella, Parmesan, onion powder, garlic powder, thyme, salt, pepper, and parsley.
4. Mist an 8 × 8-inch (roughly 20 × 20 cm) baking dish with cooking spray. Spread marinara evenly in the bottom.
5. Spread 3–4 tablespoons cheese mixture across each noodle; top with 2 tablespoons sautéed mushrooms. Roll up and place seam-side down in the dish.
6. Bake 20 minutes until golden and bubbly. Cool 10–15 minutes before serving. Garnish with fresh basil.

Rolled Mushroom Lasagna is sturdy, just like the wheels on the tour bus: built to keep rolling long after the show ends. Mushrooms may be underrated, but their earthy, meaty flavor makes this dish a total headliner. An after-party classic that proves vegetarian comfort food can rock just as hard.

CHERRY COLA BROWNIES

SERVES 12

Easy-Bake Oven, if you could see me now . . . Let's take a moment of gratitude for no longer having to bake with a 100-watt light bulb! But true statement, when I see this gorgeous, chocolatey batter, it takes me back to that moment in 1980 when I baked my first dessert in my bedroom. Maraschino cherries, cherry cola and crushed up sandwich cookies!? Sounds like Saturday night for a 10-year-old. One who will be up way past her bedtime.

INGREDIENTS

1 box fudge brownie mix (18 ounces or 520 grams)

1/2 cup cherry cola

2 large eggs

1/4 cup vegetable oil

1/2 teaspoon almond extract

1/2 cup maraschino cherries, drained, patted dry and chopped

1/2 cup crushed chocolate sandwich cookies

INSTRUCTIONS

1. Preheat oven to 350°F (177°C). Grease or line a 9 × 13-inch (roughly 23 × 33 cm) pan with parchment paper.
2. In a bowl, combine brownie mix, cherry cola, eggs, oil, and almond extract until just combined. Do not overmix.
3. Fold in chopped cherries and crushed cookies.
4. Pour into pan and smooth top. Bake 28–32 minutes until a toothpick near center comes out with a few moist crumbs.
5. Cool completely. To cut into clean squares, transfer to the freezer for 30 minutes before cutting.

Cherry Cola Brownies are pure after-party magic: fudgy, rich, and spiked with that sweet cherry-cola twist straight out of a rock 'n' roll diner. They're indulgent enough to feel rebellious, nostalgic enough to take you back, and totally savage. Dessert with a backbeat.

POPPING CANDY BARK

SERVES 10

I think we all know what "popping candy" really is. After all, it's the candy made so popular by General Foods that urban legends developed about its *dangerously cool* reputation. Chocolate bark was a bake sale darling from the 1980s onward, not to mention the confection of choice for holiday tins. This clever white chocolate version causes the most commotion at the after-party table. If they only knew how easy it is. Just melt, decorate, set, and SNAP!

INGREDIENTS

2 cups (12 ounces or 340 grams) white chocolate, chopped or chips

1/3 cup freeze-dried strawberries, crushed slightly

2 packets blue raspberry Pop Rocks

Optional garnish: edible glitter or silver stars

INSTRUCTIONS

1. Line a baking sheet with parchment paper or a silicone mat.
2. Melt white chocolate in a double boiler or microwave in 30-second bursts, stirring until smooth.
3. Cool chocolate 2–3 minutes; warm is good—hot will pop the candy.
4. Spread into a rough rectangle about 1/4-inch (roughly 1/2 cm) thick.
5. Top immediately with crushed freeze-dried strawberries and blue raspberry Pop Rocks (sprinkle just before it sets). Add glitter or stars if using.
6. Chill 30 minutes until set. Break into shards and store airtight at room temp. Keep dry—moisture kills the pop.

Popping Candy Bark is all about the fizz, loaded with Pop Rocks candy that crackle and spark like the 4th of July in your mouth. And when the ice cream truck rolled through my neighborhood in Norwalk, the kids would sprinkle Pop Rocks on top of their cones. That's exactly what I think of when I see this on the Meet & Greet table. It's colorful, playful, and proof that we're all still kids at heart.

MAPLE DONUT PUDDING

SERVES 8

Here's one for Tiffany's mom! Maple donuts were her jam, and I am right there with her. Day-old maple donuts meet a simple custard and bake into something golden at the edges and soft in the middle. And surprise! My orange zest makes another appearance in this recipe, an unmistakable harmony with any sweet bread pudding.

INGREDIENTS

2 1/2 cups half-and-half

3 large eggs

1/3 cup sugar

1 1/2 teaspoons orange zest

6 stale maple donuts, cut into 1-inch (2 1/2 cm) cubes

Nonstick cooking spray

INSTRUCTIONS

1. Preheat oven to 350°F (177°C).
2. In a large bowl, whisk half-and-half, eggs, sugar, and orange zest until blended.
3. Add donut cubes and press gently to soak; rest 5 minutes.
4. Lightly coat a loaf pan or 8 × 8-inch (roughly 20 × 20 cm) dish with cooking spray. Pour mixture in and smooth the top.
5. Bake 40–45 minutes until custard is set and the top is golden. Cool 10 minutes before serving.

Donut-based bread pudding is the ultimate late-night indulgence. It has all the comfort of warm bread pudding with the fun of maple donuts baked right in. Chef Alicia first introduced me to this dish, and I knew right away it had to be made with maple donuts. That choice was personal: my mom, Janie, was a huge donut lover, and maple was her favorite. Every year in remembrance of her, my whole family heads to the donut shop, and this recipe now carries that same joy and love in every gooey, sweet bite.

THAI TURKEY SLIDERS

YIELDS 8 SLIDERS

Juicy turkey patties scented with ginger, lemongrass, and herbs, finished with a swipe of the same bold mixture on top. Soft buns, cool greens, a bite of onion . . . big flavor without the weight. When Tiffany isn't touring in Southeast Asia, she prepares these to remind her of the wonderful people she's met in that part of the world. And sliders are always a hit at parties. Bet you can't eat just one!

INGREDIENTS

1/2 teaspoon garlic salt

4 teaspoons garlic powder

1 teaspoons ground black pepper

4 teaspoons freshly grated ginger

16 teaspoons jarred mango ginger chutney

2 teaspoons dried minced onion

2 teaspoons dried basil

1 teaspoons Worcestershire sauce

4 teaspoon lemongrass paste

4 teaspoons Thai seasoning paste

1 pound (453 grams) ground turkey

8 brioche slider buns

1/4 cup chopped fresh cilantro, for garnish

2 teaspoon chopped fresh mint, for garnish

Small red onion, sliced into 8 thin rings

Green leaf lettuce

INSTRUCTIONS

1. In a bowl, combine garlic salt, garlic powder, black pepper, ginger, mango ginger chutney, dried onion, basil, Worcestershire sauce, lemongrass paste, and Thai seasoning paste until thick and even. Divide into two bowls.
2. Reserve half of the seasoning mixture and transfer the other half to a medium bowl with the ground turkey. Mix the ground turkey, until all ingredients are evenly distributed. Form 8 slider patties.
3. Sear patties 4–6 minutes per side until cooked through and internal temperature reaches 165°F (74°C).
4. After flipping the burgers, spread 1–2 teaspoons of the reserved seasoning mixture on each patty.
5. Place each patty on a bun, seasoned side up. Add cilantro-mint garnish, one onion ring, and a piece of green leaf lettuce. Cap with the top bun and serve.

Thai Turkey Sliders bring a taste of my favorite getaway straight to the after party. Thailand is the land of smiles, and every bite of these sliders, with their bold, bright flavors, takes me back to relaxing days at The Banyan Tree. Making them at home feels like bringing a little piece of my favorite tour stop back with me. Hours of flavor with a first-class stamp.

MANGO GINGER CHUTNEY

SERVES 12

Looking for an extra dollop on your Thai Turkey Sliders? We thought so. Tiffany loves a good chutney and this is one of her finest. Sweet, tangy mango balanced with warm ginger, a hint of heat, earthy cumin, and a bright splash of lime, with just enough vinegar to keep it poppin'. It's one of those condiments that instantly zhuzhes up anything it touches: grilled chicken, cheese boards, even a simple sandwich.

INGREDIENTS

3 cups diced fresh mango

1 cup granulated sugar

1/3 cup golden raisins

1/4 cup finely diced red bell pepper

1/4 cup finely diced onion

1 1/2 teaspoon freshly grated ginger

1/4 cup apple cider vinegar

1 tablespoon fresh lime juice

1/4 teaspoon sea salt

1/2 teaspoon ground cumin

1/8 teaspoon red pepper flakes

INSTRUCTIONS

1. Add all ingredients to a medium saucepan and bring to a gentle boil over medium-high heat.
2. Reduce heat to medium and simmer, stirring frequently, until the mixture starts to thicken, about 20 - 25 minutes.
3. Cook until the mango softens and the mixture thickens into a spoonable chutney.
4. Cool slightly before serving or storing.

I'm obsessed with this chutney because it's so versatile. I've spooned it over the Thai Turkey Sliders, crackers, used it as a glaze on salmon, and even paired it with scrambled eggs. It's bold without being overpowering, and it always makes people ask, "What is that?" To me, that's the sign of a recipe worth keeping. I love how it takes humble ingredients and turns them into something that feels special and a little unexpected.

Vegas Residency

- BBQ CHICKEN FRENCH BREAD PIZZA
- CLAMS CASINO CROSTINO
- QUESO FUNDIDO MAC & CHEESE
- CREAMY SPINACH AND ARTICHOKE CAULIFLOWER
- MINI MAC TOTS
- TABBOULEH
- GARDEN TZATZIKI AND CRUDITÉS
- SWEDISH MEATLOAF
- MINI ARAYES
- CHAI RAISIN ROLLS
- DENVER SHEET BREAKFAST

A residency is about roots. The stage doesn't move, but the audience does, finding its way back to you again and again. During my residency at the Las Vegas Hilton in the 90s, I learned how magical that rhythm could be. It wasn't about arenas or pyrotechnics; it was about intimacy. The room wasn't massive, but the connection was. I could see faces, hear voices singing every word, and step right off the stage into the crowd. Those nights taught me that a residency isn't just about performing. It's about belonging.

That same spirit runs through my friendship with Chef Alicia. When I come to Vegas now, her home becomes my second residency. Her husband, Mark, an incredible artist and former musician, drifts in from their garage/art studio with paint on his hands and a huge hug for me. Their English bulldog, Belma, trots through the kitchen with a toy, and the vibe is everything I need between shows. Chef Alicia opens a bottle of wine, and everything else fades away. It's our time together, and, of course, after we toast, we immediately start cooking.

Chef Alicia specializes in original recipes for two, but we both have very healthy appetites. So, I don't suggest that we adhere only to recipes for two when we're together. Chef Alicia is used to cooking for 50 to 60 people at a time! But when I visit her in Las Vegas, there are some must-have favorites that I adore, and I know you will, too. These recipes are personal, nostalgic, and sometimes indulgent. Chef Alicia is Queen of the Mashups, so there are quite a few 80s dishes you'll likely recognize, zhuzhed up in the most delicious ways.

In my teens, my parents allowed me to move from our home in Norwalk to Hollywood, just up the freeway. I lived with my manager and was invited to parties and premiers every week. It was an awesome time to be in LA, especially for food. In 1982, Wolfgang Puck debuted his famous BBQ Chicken Pizza at Spago, his flagship restaurant in Los Angeles. In Chef Alicia's BBQ Chicken French Bread Pizza, this iconic dish collides with frozen French bread pizza, a snack so many of us enjoyed as kids. It's unfussy but dramatic in its own way: golden French bread piled with tender chicken, smothered in tangy BBQ sauce under a blanket of melted cheese. It's bold, messy, and can be center stage on any table.

Attend enough of Chef Alicia's events and you will come to appreciate how she can fit just about anything on a crostino- she was the one who informed me that crostino is singular for crostini. A lyricist in her own unique way, she gets very excited when her recipes rhyme. So, I had to include her recipe for Clams Casino Crostino, which takes a retro classic—clams baked with butter, bacon, and breadcrumbs—and perches it on a crispy sliced baguette. Handheld, dramatic, glitzy, smoky . . . Heaven. Unapologetically bold and a little indulgent but still anchored in Vegas tradition.

Then comes Queso Fundido Mac & Cheese; to *die* for! Chef Alicia and I love our Tex-Mex food, as you've come to know by now. "Queso fundido" literally means "melted cheese," and it traditionally features melted cheese and chorizo, and is served with tortillas. In the 80s, some of the most popular Mexican restaurant chains started to serve queso fundido, which is the culinary equivalent to the highly processed "queso dip" that has become an American staple. And why wouldn't Chef Alicia mash up this Tex-Mex treasure with mac and cheese? Exactly.

Next, we dazzle you with another mashup: Creamy Spinach and Artichoke Cauliflower. Chef Alicia is originally from Silicon Valley, and boy, do they love their sourdough! If you were at any party in the 80s, chances are you remember diving into a hollowed out, round of sourdough, filled with Spinach and Artichoke Dip that was warm, savory and delicious. Just to prove that we do eat our veggies when I am in Vegas, I chose Chef Alicia's Creamy Spinach and Artichoke Cauliflower, which is a spectacular combination of the oh-so-popular riced cauliflower, and proves that vegetables can headline too. It's rich but not heavy, the perfect side for two.

And then there are Mini Mac Tots, Chef Alicia's homage to the Golden Arches. Yes, we did love our fast food as kids. It was a treat for both of us, and not something we were allowed to eat on a regular basis. And when we're feeling extra naughty, Chef Alicia will make a full batch of these (extra portions welcomed), which resemble the perfect hand-held burger and fries two-bite combo.

One thing I appreciate most about Chef Alicia is her love of balance. With Tabbouleh, she reaches back into my heritage to honor my Lebanese roots. I taught her how to make it right: more parsley than you think you need, lots of lemon, and extra-fine bulgur. It's fresh and clean, the palate reset you need when the rest of the table leans heavy. And when we are in a Tabbouleh mood, we love to double down with Garden Tzatziki and Crudités; they're cool, crisp, and refreshing, proof that glamour can be as simple as a cucumber dipped in garlicky yogurt.

When we were kids, it was popular to add dehydrated onion soup mix to ground beef and bake it for meatloaf. It was average and to be honest, not very memorable. So, when Chef Alicia let me taste her Swedish Meatloaf, I was hooked. Remember how everyone's faces lit up when the cool mom busted out a slow cooker filled with creamy, delicious Swedish meatballs? There were never enough of them, and before you knew it, all that was left was thick, goopy gravy, just bubbling away. Swedish Meatloaf takes everything you probably dislike about meatloaf and scales up for a fun retro main any night of the week. And because it's a full loaf, you get dinner for two *and* enough for sandwiches the next day.

When I see Chef Alicia grab a bag of mini pitas out of the pantry, I know it's time for Mini Arayes, one of the appetizers she made for her longstanding culinary residency in Las Vegas. What we love about them is that you can make a few arayes or a few platters of arayes, and they are always a hit: mini pita pockets, stuffed with spiced meat and grilled until crisp. Another nod to my Lebanese roots. Eating them in Chef Alicia's kitchen always makes me feel like I've carried a piece of my family into hers.

In the morning, we are usually up for something sweet, and that's where Chai Raisin Rolls shine. Warm spices swirl through the dough, studded with raisins, and I feel like I am in the middle of an Indian bakery. Denver Sheet Breakfast has the same easy charm and trust me, I am never going back to making Denver omelets after learning Chef Alicia's sheet pan technique.

What ties all of these recipes together is the balance of sparkle and comfort, of friendship and showmanship. A residency is about showing up again and again, finding new ways to keep the magic alive. That's exactly what these dishes do. They're familiar but reimagined, comforting but elevated, nostalgic yet forward-looking.

For me, Vegas will always mean both sequins and sweatpants, neon lights and quiet mornings, over-the-top shows and humble meals shared with friends. This chapter is my way of honoring all of it, from the sparkle of the Strip to our laughter in Chef Alicia's kitchen. These are the recipes that remind me why coming back to Sin City always feels like coming home.

CHEF'S TIPS—VEGAS RESIDENCY

This chapter blends showmanship with comfort—familiar flavors, thoughtful technique, and results you can count on. The key is *mindfulness*: managing texture, temperature, and proportion so each dish feels intentional but easy to make.

1. PORTION RICH DISHES THOUGHTFULLY

Applies to: Queso Fundido Mac & Cheese, Creamy Spinach and Artichoke Cauliflower, Swedish Meatloaf

Smaller portions make rich dishes more satisfying. Serve them in shallow bowls or small ramekins, then top with herbs or microgreens for a lighter, more composed finish.

2. BUILD CRISP TEXTURE WITHOUT OVERBAKING

Applies to: BBQ Chicken French Bread Pizza, Mini Mac Tots, Clams Casino Crostino

For oven-based recipes, start with a properly preheated surface; a hot baking sheet or stone promotes crispness from the bottom up. Avoid crowding and finish briefly under the broiler for color if needed. Rest items for a few minutes before cutting to prevent sogginess.

3. HANDLE MOISTURE IN VEGETABLE-BASED DISHES

Applies to: Creamy Spinach and Artichoke Cauliflower, Tabbouleh, Garden Tzatziki and Crudités

Vegetables release water as they cook or sit. Drain, blot, or salt in advance to reduce excess moisture. For cold salads and dips, mix dressing or yogurt at the last minute to maintain freshness and prevent separation.

4. MANAGE PORTION SIZE FOR CLEAN PRESENTATION

Applies to: Mini Arayes, Clams Casino Crostino, Denver Sheet Breakfast

Miniature or multi-bite items benefit from consistency. Use a scoop, ring mold, or even spacing to ensure uniform cooking. Keep portions small enough for easy serving but large enough to hold structure without crumbling.

5. CONTROL DOUGH AND BATTER TEMPERATURE

Applies to: Chai Raisin Rolls, Denver Sheet Breakfast

Yeast and leavening respond best to room-temperature ingredients. Avoid overmixing; gentle handling preserves tenderness. Allow baked goods to cool before glazing or dusting so toppings adhere cleanly without melting.

BACKSTAGE TAKEAWAY

These recipes are built on contrast—rich yet fresh, precise yet relaxed. Pay attention to moisture, heat, and seasoning. When each element complements the others, the result feels both polished and natural.

BBQ CHICKEN FRENCH BREAD PIZZA

SERVES 2

Remember the frozen French bread pizzas we all begged for and the 80s BBQ chicken pizza craze? This version honors the sentimentality of both in one hand-held appetizer. Sweet, tangy sauce, stretchy mozzarella, and soft peppers make it feel like a night off, even when we're still in sequins. It's the perfect couch supper for two with a glass of wine and a good debrief after the show.

INGREDIENTS

1/2 loaf French bread

2 tablespoons melted butter

2 teaspoons olive oil

1 cup thinly sliced yellow and red bell peppers

1/4 teaspoon salt

1 cup cooked, shredded chicken breast

1/4 cup barbecue sauce

1 cup shredded mozzarella cheese

2 tablespoons chopped cilantro

INSTRUCTIONS

1. Preheat oven to 400°F (204°C). Split the half loaf lengthwise, into 2 pieces, and transfer to a baking sheet lined with parchment paper.
2. Brush cut sides with melted butter and bake 5 minutes, until lightly toasted.
3. Reduce oven temperature to 350°F (177°C).
4. In a medium skillet, sauté peppers in olive oil over medium heat; season with salt. When tender, after about 5 minutes, transfer the peppers to a bowl.
5. In a separate bowl, combine chicken and barbecue sauce.
6. To assemble the first BBQ Chicken French Bread Pizza, layer half the sautéed peppers, followed by 1/4 cup of shredded cheese, half of the BBQ chicken, and top with 1/4 cup cheese. Repeat to assemble the second BBQ French Bread Pizza.
7. Bake 5–10 minutes until the cheese is melted and bubbling.
8. To serve, garnish with cilantro.

BBQ Chicken French bread pizza is Vegas comfort turned all the way up: smoky chicken, tangy sauce, and bubbling cheese piled sky-high on golden French bread. It's a taste of California, but big and bold enough to keep the after-hours crowd satisfied. From California to the Strip, flavor takes the stage.

CLAMS CASINO CROSTINO

SERVES 2

Old-school casino flavor on my precious crostini: smoky bacon, sweet peppers, and buttery clams under a little Parmesan. They bake fast, hold up on a platter, and feel like neon lights in snack form. And thanks to canned clams, which are making a huge comeback, there are no messy, stinky shells to get in our way.

INGREDIENTS

2 tablespoons unsalted butter

2 slices bacon, diced finely

1/4 cup diced mini sweet peppers

2 tablespoons diced onion

2 tablespoons grated Parmesan cheese

1 teaspoon chopped parsley

1/4 teaspoon dried oregano

Pinch of black pepper

1 tablespoon breadcrumbs

2 ounces (56 grams) canned clams, drained and minced

6 baguette slices, 1/4-inch (roughly 1/2 cm) thick

1 tablespoon olive oil

Pinch of salt

Lemon wedges, for serving

INSTRUCTIONS

1. Preheat oven to 400°F (204°C). Melt butter over medium heat; sauté bacon 3 minutes.
2. Add peppers and onions. Reduce heat to medium low and cook 8–10 minutes, until soft.
3. Off heat, stir in Parmesan cheese, parsley, oregano, pepper, breadcrumbs, and clams.
4. Transfer mixture to a bowl and refrigerate for 30 minutes.
5. Brush baguette slices with olive oil, sprinkle with salt, and toast 6 minutes.
6. Reduce oven temperature to 375°F (190°C).
7. Mound an equal amount of clam mixture onto each toasted baguette slice. Bake 8–10 minutes, until the baguette crisps and the clam mixture is lightly browned.
8. Serve with lemon wedges.

Clams Casino Crostino is pure Rat Pack energy: smoky clams, buttery breadcrumbs, and just enough bacon to feel indulgent. Served on crisp crostini, it's the kind of appetizer you'd imagine in a velvet booth with a martini in hand, the neon buzzing outside. Old-school Vegas flavor with a showbiz smile.

Queso fundido meets mac and cheese in a dish that shines as bright as the Vegas Strip. Oozy, cheesy, and built for indulgence, this recipe is pure showtime comfort, the kind of headliner you want on your table. Inspired by Chef Alicia, a true star of the Vegas Kitchen stage, it's mac with the Midas touch.

QUESO FUNDIDO MAC & CHEESE

SERVES 2

The famous skillet dip flips into a creamy, bubbling mac built for two. Chorizo brings the sizzle, Oaxaca cheese melts like a dream, and a little spice keeps things humming. It's rich but not heavy, exactly the comfort we want when the night still has stories left. Don't see spicy Mexican breadcrumbs at your local grocery store? Substitute fine breadcrumbs and add a teaspoon of my Distilled Spices Al Pastor, or your favorite spicy taco seasoning.

INGREDIENTS

3 1/2 ounces (100 grams) small pasta shells

3 ounces (85 grams) pork chorizo

1/2 cup pico de gallo, drained + 2 tablespoons, for garnish

2 teaspoons minced jalapeño

1/2 teaspoon minced garlic

1 teaspoon taco seasoning

2 tablespoons flour

1/2 cup Mexican crema + 2 tablespoons for garnish

3/4 cup milk

3/4 cup (3 ounces or 84 grams) Oaxaca cheese, shredded

Nonstick cooking spray

1/4 cup spicy Mexican breadcrumbs

INSTRUCTIONS

1. Cook pasta 2 minutes shy of package directions; drain.
2. Preheat oven to 350°F (177°C).
3. Brown chorizo in a skillet over medium heat. Transfer chorizo to a paper towel-lined plate to drain, leaving 1 teaspoon fat in skillet.
4. Sauté drained pico de gallo, jalapeño, garlic, and taco seasoning over medium-low heat for 3 minutes. Sprinkle in flour; cook 1 minute.
5. Slowly whisk in the crema and milk. Increase heat to medium and simmer 3–4 minutes, until slightly thickened.
6. Fold in half the chorizo and the pasta.
7. Whisk in 1/2 cup (2 ounces or 56 grams) Oaxaca cheese, stirring frequently, until melted.
8. Apply a thin coating of nonstick spray to a small baking dish.
9. Transfer mac and cheese to the prepared baking dish. Top with remaining chorizo, remaining Oaxaca cheese, and breadcrumbs. Drizzle the top with remaining 2 tablespoons crema.
10. Bake 20–25 minutes until bubbling. Garnish with reserved pico de gallo.

CREAMY SPINACH AND ARTICHOKE CAULIFLOWER

SERVES 2

All the flavors of the classic party dip, baked into a creamy side that soothes the soul. Riced cauliflower keeps it light; Parmesan and Boursin keep it luxe. And when we're really sassy, we drop our forks and shovel it onto tortilla chips.

INGREDIENTS

Nonstick cooking spray

2 tablespoons cream cheese

2 teaspoons sour cream

2 teaspoons mayonnaise

2 tablespoons grated Parmesan cheese

1 ounce (28 grams) Boursin or herbed goat cheese

1/4 teaspoon salt

1/4 teaspoon black pepper

3 ounces (85 grams) frozen riced cauliflower, thawed and squeezed dry

1 ounce (28 grams) marinated artichoke hearts, chopped

3 ounces (85 grams) frozen spinach, thawed and squeezed dry

INSTRUCTIONS

1. Preheat oven to 350°F (177°C). Apply a thin layer of cooking spray to a small baking dish.
2. In a large bowl, combine cream cheese, sour cream, mayonnaise, Parmesan, Boursin, salt, and pepper, until smooth.
3. Fold in cauliflower, artichokes, and spinach.
4. Transfer mixture to the prepared baking dish and bake 20 minutes, until hot and lightly golden.

This creamy spinach and artichoke cauliflower is a Vegas-worthy remix of a classic dip, rich, decadent, and dazzling enough to feel like a headliner. It's comfort food with a spotlight twist, the kind of dish that keeps the crowd coming back for more. With Chef Alicia's touch, it's a jackpot of flavor.

Mini Mac Tots are the bite-sized gamble that always pays off: crispy Tater Tots stuffed with scrumptious ground beef, baked until golden and ready for the Strip. They're flashy, naughty, and built to keep the party rolling long after the final curtain call. When I want a new twist on these at home, I brown chorizo and mix with it hot sauce for a Tex-Mex version.

MINI MAC TOTS

SERVES 6

Some recipes should never be downsized. These tiny Tater Tots cups hold seasoned beef, melty cheese, and burger sauce so perfectly that we make the full batch and call it a win. They're grab-and-grin food, a little crispy, a little saucy, and very hard to stop eating. Perfect for neighbors dropping by or for us two, pretending it's a party.

INGREDIENTS

1 pound (453 grams) ground beef

1 teaspoon garlic salt

1/2 teaspoon pepper

1/2 cup finely diced onion

2 tablespoons mayonnaise

2 tablespoons yellow mustard

2 tablespoons ketchup

2 tablespoons dill pickle relish

Nonstick cooking spray

48 frozen Tater Tots (or similar)

1 cup shredded cheddar cheese

Additional ketchup and mustard, for serving

INSTRUCTIONS

1. Preheat oven to 425°F (218°C).
2. Cook beef in a skillet over medium high heat, 3–4 minutes. Season with garlic salt and pepper.
3. Add onion and cook 3–4 minutes, until onions are tender and beef is browned. Off heat, stir in mayonnaise, mustard, ketchup, and relish.
4. Spray a mini muffin pan with a thin layer of cooking spray. Put 2 frozen tots in each cup; bake 10 minutes.
5. Remove the pan from the oven and carefully use a spoon to press the tots to form individual cups.
6. Fill each cup with a couple teaspoons of beef mixture, then top with a sprinkle of cheese.
7. Bake 15 minutes.
8. Cool Mini Mac Tots in the pan for 5 minutes before transferring them to a platter to serve.
9. Garnish with a drizzle of ketchup and mustard.

TABBOULEH

SERVES 2

Tiffany and I served this recipe for our first event together in Las Vegas. I love to have it ready for her every time she visits. Bold, lemony, and herb-forward, we use extra-fine bulgur with a ton of parsley, fresh mint, tomatoes, and green onions. Two forks, one bowl. Then the gossip begins.

INGREDIENTS

2 tablespoons extra-fine bulgur wheat

1 tablespoon lemon juice

2 tablespoons extra virgin olive oil

1/2 cup finely chopped curly parsley

1 small tomato, cored, seeded, and diced

1 green onion, sliced thinly

2 tablespoons chopped fresh mint

1/4 teaspoon salt

1/4 teaspoon pepper

INSTRUCTIONS

1. In a large bowl, pour boiling water over bulgur. Cover and let stand until tender, about 20–25 minutes. Fluff with a fork and let cool.
2. Whisk lemon juice and olive oil in a small bowl.
3. Finely chop parsley, tomato, green onion, and mint. Drain excess tomato juice if needed.
4. Combine vegetables in a large bowl. Add bulgur and dressing and toss gently.
5. Season with salt and pepper.
6. Refrigerate for 30 minutes before serving.

Tabbouleh is one of my Lebanese classics, fresh, vibrant, and exploding with flavor. I remember making it with Chef Alicia while hanging out in Vegas, and it always connects me back to my roots. The parsley and lemon take me straight to memories of my Lebanese grandmother, while Vegas reminds me of the years I lived there with my dad and called it home during my live music residency there.

GARDEN TZATZIKI AND CRUDITÉS

SERVES 2

Cool yogurt, crunchy veggies, and a little cream cheese for luxe texture, this dip is our greenroom at home. The dill and mint make it fresh, the cumin keeps it cozy, and the colorful crudités make it feel like a platter even when it's just us two. Leftovers (if any) are perfect on grilled chicken or tucked into a pita.

INGREDIENTS

1/2 large seedless cucumber, shredded and well-squeezed

1 cup plain full-fat Greek yogurt

1/4 cup (2 ounces or 56 grams) cream cheese

1 tablespoon minced red onion

1 tablespoon minced yellow bell pepper

1 small garlic clove, grated finely

1 teaspoon chopped fresh dill

2 tablespoons chopped fresh mint

1/2 teaspoon ground cumin

1/4 teaspoon kosher salt

1/4 teaspoon black pepper

For serving:

Assorted crudités, pita chips, or naan bread

INSTRUCTIONS

1. Combine all ingredients in a bowl until smooth and creamy.
2. Chill at least 1 hour to let flavors marry. Serve with a rainbow of vegetables, pita chips, or warm naan.

Garden Tzatziki and Crudites is the kind of cool, refreshing opener every Vegas show needs. Creamy, with herby garden flavors, it's the snack I reach for at special events when I need to stay healthy and fueled before stepping in front of the camera or hitting the stage. Fresh, crisp, and endlessly snackable.

SWEDISH MEATLOAF

SERVES 6

A cozy mash-up of meatloaf and Swedish meatballs, finished with a lingonberry glaze and a silky gravy. It's generous, nostalgic, and kind, the sort of dish that makes the room exhale. We keep this one full-sized on purpose because the next-day sandwich is half the thrill. Slice thick, warm the gravy, and call it brunch if you want. We do.

INGREDIENTS

Meatloaf:

2 1/2 cups chopped onions

1 tablespoon minced garlic

1 tablespoon olive oil

2 teaspoons salt

1/4 teaspoon black pepper

1 pound (453 grams) ground beef

1 pound (453 grams) ground pork

1 tablespoon chopped Italian parsley

3 tablespoons Worcestershire sauce

1/3 cup milk

1/2 cup plain breadcrumbs

2 eggs, beaten

1/2 teaspoon ground allspice

1/2 teaspoon ground ginger

1/4 teaspoon ground nutmeg

1/4 cup lingonberry preserves

1/4 cup ketchup

Gravy:

3 tablespoons butter

3 tablespoons flour

1 teaspoon thyme

1/4 teaspoon allspice

1 tablespoon Dijon mustard

2 cups beef broth

1/2 cup cream

2 teaspoons Worcestershire sauce

1/4 teaspoon salt

1/2 teaspoon pepper

2 tablespoons chopped parsley, for garnish

INSTRUCTIONS

1. Preheat oven to 325°F (163°C). Cook onion and garlic in olive oil with salt and pepper until soft; cool slightly.
2. Combine meats, parsley, Worcestershire sauce, milk, breadcrumbs, eggs, spices, and onion mixture. Mix gently.
3. Shape into a loaf on a lined sheet. Blend lingonberry preserves with ketchup; spread over loaf.
4. Bake 60–65 minutes or until 165°F (74°C) internal temperature.
5. For gravy, melt butter; whisk in flour and cook 1–2 minutes. Add thyme, allspice, and Dijon mustard; whisk in broth. Simmer to thicken, then add cream and Worcestershire sauce. Season to taste.
6. Slice and serve with gravy; garnish with parsley.

I love the tastes of Sweden. It's food that keeps you warm at night and feels like a hug on a plate. I've always been a huge fan of meatloaf, but after Chef Alicia showed me how to make it Swedish-style, I just can't stop making it. Hearty, savory, and layered with creamy flavors that hit all the right notes, this dish takes classic comfort and gives it a Vegas stage presence. A showstopper that brings down the house, bite after bite.

MINI ARAYES

SERVES 2

A street-food favorite scaled to bite size: mini pita pockets stuffed with spiced beef, pressed on a grill pan until the outside is crisp and the inside stays juicy. They're fast, fragrant, and perfect with a squeeze of lemon or a swipe of tahini yogurt. My favorite thing is to fire up a batch and listen to Tiffany's stories about the parties she went to in the 80s.

INGREDIENTS

1 teaspoon olive oil

1 tablespoon minced onion

1 teaspoon za'atar seasoning blend

2 teaspoons tahini

1/4 cup Greek yogurt

1 teaspoon lemon juice

1 tablespoon finely chopped parsley

4 ounces (roughly 133 grams) lean ground beef

8 mini pita

1/4 teaspoon salt

INSTRUCTIONS

1. Sauté onion with half the za'atar in olive oil 2–3 minutes; cool.
2. Stir together tahini, yogurt, and lemon juice; set aside for dipping.
3. Mix cooled onion with remaining za'atar, parsley, and beef. Season lightly with salt.
4. Slice one end of each pita and stuff with beef, pressing filling flat and to the edges.
5. Brush outside with a little oil and cook in a hot grill pan or panini press 2–3 minutes per side.
6. Serve warm with tahini sauce.

Mini Arayes are Lebanese street food with a Vegas twist: crisp pita pockets stuffed with spiced meat that deliver big flavor in every bite. They're sizzling, savory, and perfect for passing around when the crowd wants something bold and shareable. A high-roller snack with Middle Eastern soul.

CHAI RAISIN ROLLS

SERVES 2

Don't get it twisted. Actually, do. Pizza dough becomes spiced breakfast buns with a chai-sugar swirl and a little rum-kissed glaze. They perfume the kitchen and make a slow morning feel like a holiday. We bake just two so there's no pressure, only pleasure.

INGREDIENTS

Chai raisin rolls:

7 ounces (198 grams) refrigerated pizza dough

2 1/2 tablespoons melted butter

1/4 cup sugar

1 1/2 teaspoons masala chai

1/4 cup raisins

Glaze:

1/2 cup powdered sugar

1 tablespoon milk

1/8 teaspoon rum extract

INSTRUCTIONS

1. Preheat oven to 400°F (204°C). Roll half the dough into a 10 × 7-inch (25 × 18 cm) rectangle.
2. Brush with 1 1/2 tablespoons butter. Mix sugar with masala chai and sprinkle over, reserving a pinch.
3. Scatter raisins over the lower half; fold lengthwise, seal edges, twist into a rope, and coil into a bun. Repeat for second roll.
4. Brush tops with remaining butter; dust with reserved chai sugar. Bake 20–25 minutes until golden.
5. Whisk powdered sugar, milk, and rum extract; drizzle over warm rolls.

Chai Raisin Rolls are sweet, spiced, and just what I need to recharge the morning after a show. The chai brings a fragrant kick and the raisins add that classic chew. Not your average cinnamon roll.

DENVER SHEET BREAKFAST

SERVES 2

All the diner vibes, none of the dishes. Cheese melts into a lacy base, while eggs bake sunny right on top, with ham and peppers scattered like confetti. It slices into neat squares you can eat with a fork or tuck into toast. Perfect for late mornings after late nights.

INGREDIENTS

1/4 cup (2 ounces or 56 grams) shredded cheddar cheese

2 eggs

1 1/2 ounces (43 grams) ham, chopped

2 tablespoons diced bell peppers

A few thin slices red onion

Pinch of salt

1 green onion, sliced, for garnish

INSTRUCTIONS

1. Preheat oven to 375°F (190°C). Line a small sheet pan with parchment paper.
2. Spread cheese in an even layer. Clear two small circles and crack an egg into each.
3. Scatter ham, peppers, and onion around whites; season yolks lightly with salt.
4. Bake 10–12 minutes until eggs are set to your liking. Cool 5 minutes, then cut into squares and garnish with green onion.

Denver Sheet Breakfast takes all the goodness of a Denver omelet and super-sizes it for the Vegas stage. Sunny-side up eggs, peppers, onions, and ham baked into one big crowd pleaser, perfect for when the sun comes up quicker than you realize, and you're still rockin' but it's breakfast time. Breakfast with big city lights energy.

Pop Lifestyle

Tiffany and Chef Alicia make life pop! From spices to cocktails and fashion to wellness, they've each built lifestyle brands you can taste, wear, join, and share, extensions of their creativity that bring *Pop Life* off the page and into everyday living.

TIFFANY

Tiffany first expanded her artistry into food during the pandemic with Tiff Takeovers, intimate evenings where fans could taste her cooking and then hear her sing. That spark evolved into Let's Food with Tiffany, a cooking club that continues to invite fans into her kitchen and celebrate her Lebanese roots alongside flavors she has collected from years on tour.

She went on to create a Spice Trio: Rockstar Za'atar, Hip Hop Harissa, and Let's Taco Taco Taco. Each is bold, playful, and distinctly Tiffany, giving fans a way to bring her personality to their own tables.

With Poptails, developed in collaboration with celebrity mixologist Rob Floyd, she extended her lifestyle brand into cocktails. Fans could now mix, sip, and celebrate Tiffany's flavor beyond the stage.

Beyond food and drink, Tiffany launched Radikal Redz, a boutique of clothing and accessories that captures her fearless, expressive style. She also created Let's Zen My Friend, a wellness-focused lifestyle community that promotes balance and intentional living. Each venture reflects a different side of Tiffany's world, together forming a lifestyle brand that resonates across kitchens, wardrobes, and wellness routines.

CHEF ALICIA

Chef Alicia's lifestyle brand began with Dink Cuisine, a food and entertainment platform built around right-sized cooking for two. Through dinkcuisine.com, she has reached audiences in more than 100 countries, inspiring couples, roommates, empty nesters, and duos of all flavors to cook smaller, and smarter.

Her Distilled Spices line grew from a playful tequila salt gift at a SAHARA Las Vegas pop-up into a full collection of spirit-inspired blends. Flavors like Limoncello Pepper, Manhattan BBQ, French Onion, and Pomodoro can be found in international airports, regional retailers, and in kitchens across the country. Distilled Spices inspired a wholesale line of elevated bar snacks, featured at resorts and properties on the Las Vegas Strip.

Chef Alicia has authored three cookbooks: *Italian Cookbook for Two, Vegetarian Ketogenic Cookbook for Beginners*, and *Food With Spirit.* Each title reflects her blend of practicality, playfulness, and storytelling through food. Her pop-up events remain a signature, transforming unexpected spaces into immersive experiences where delectable food, stories, and guests come together in unforgettable ways.

TOGETHER

Tiffany and Chef Alicia's worlds first overlapped in February 2023 at The Space in Las Vegas, for their first co-branded event. An entirely new spin on Tiffany's successful Tiff Takeovers, Chef Alicia Presents: An Evening with Tiffany featured a Mediterranean menu they created together, followed by an explosive performance from Tiffany to a sold-out crowd. In a moment of pure

spontaneity, Tiffany pulled Chef Alicia out from the kitchen and onto the stage to announce, unscripted, that they were writing this cookbook together. It was unexpected, joyful, and the spark for everything that followed.

Fans can expect more of these events in the future, each one a new way to experience *Pop Life* live, off the page, and in unforgettable company. These events are more than dinner theater; they are immersive evenings where food and music share the same spotlight.

Placed side by side, their brands reveal a natural harmony. Together, their ventures form a lifestyle as bold as this book itself.

Pop Life is only the beginning. Expect more music, more culinary mashups, and more moments designed to sparkle long after the night is over. See you at the next show!

TIFFANY THEN...
Back in the day on
The Mall Tour
The New Inside era
The Color Of Silence era
My high school photo
Outside my Tustin
home on my bike
First head shot
age 11
Me and my dog
Raider age 17
Me in my home in
Tustin, California 90's
...AND NOW
Me at Blackbird Studio
in Nashville chillin
Current photo me at Blackbird
Studio in Nashville
NYC behind the scenes
fashion shoot
CHILDREN
BEHAVE
Wearing my favorite t-shirt
I Think We're Alone Now video
shoot 2019 at Venice Beach
Angels photo shoot
2025 the classic selfie
My chef jacket getting
ready for a Let's Food With
Tiffany event

TIFFANY'S FAVORITE THINGS
isy my dog
Finishing projects with my favorite champagne
Meditating in beautiful surroundings - this is in France
My spice blends which I'm very proud of
Girl lunches
The Cavern Club in Liverpool
CAVERN CLUB
Intimate acoustic shows with Mark
Holiday dinners with my family
Christmas time at my home with my Kit Kat
Sunsets at my house
My closet and growing my shoe collection
Finishing the cookbook
Rocking a stage everywhere
THE LANGHAM
The beach
The Langham Hotel in London
Having beautiful flowers around me

Encore Bonus Track

WHAT WOULD AN 80s BOOK BE WITHOUT A *TEEN BEAT*–STYLE Q&A? TIFFANY AND CHEF ALICIA WEIGH IN ON THEIR 80S FAVES . . .

Q: What is your favorite '80s movie?
Tiffany: Jaws
Chef Alicia: Pee-wee's Big Adventure

Q: What was the first cassette you ever bought?
Tiffany: Van Halen
Chef Alicia: Thriller

Q: Aqua Net or mousse?
Tiffany: Aqua Net
Chef Alicia: Aqua Net

Q: Who was your favorite 80s dream bedroom poster?
Tiffany: Eddie Van Halen
Chef Alicia: I wasn't allowed posters in the 80s . . . stupid wallpaper!

Q: What was your favorite 80s TV show?
Tiffany: MTV
Chef Alicia: Headbangers Ball

Q: Horror, Teen Romance, or Sci-Fi?
Tiffany: Sci-Fi
Chef Alicia: Sci-Fi

Q: What was your absolute favorite 80s snack food?
Tiffany: Cheez-Its
Chef Alicia: Cheetos

Q: Which 80s fashion trend needs a comeback, and which one should stay gone?
Tiffany: Comeback: long sweaters / Stay gone: leg warmers
Chef Alicia: Comeback: oversized blazers with shoulder pads / Stay gone: perms

Q: What 80s artist or band were you most excited to meet?
Tiffany: Michael Jackson (I even have a photo!)
Chef Alicia: Tiffany, of course!

Q: Fonzie, David Bowie, or Tom Selleck?
Tiffany: David Bowie
Chef Alicia: Can I choose Matt Houston??

Q: What was your favorite store in the mall?
Tiffany: Charlotte Russe
Chef Alicia: Contempo Casuals

Q: If your kitchen had a mixtape, what's the first track?
Tiffany: Simple Minds: "Don't You (Forget About Me)"
Chef Alicia: Sweet Sensation: "Hooked on You"

A GIFT FOR YOU

As a thank-you for supporting Pop Life, scan the QR code to download two new songs, Tiffany's exclusive companion tracks for the cookbook!

ACKNOWLEDGMENTS

FROM TIFFANY:

I'd like to thank my family for always believing in me and helping me achieve my dreams. And for all their love.

To Elijah, my son who makes me proud every day to be his mom and grateful for all the wonderful memories we share over food and laughter. Love you.

To Team Tiff for all the behind-the-scenes work they put into Tiff world to make it all happen. I love you guys.

To Chef Alicia for being a great mentor to me and a wonderful friend. I'm grateful for all the fun we share and the new opportunities to travel for cooking events and build a worldwide foodie community.

A special thank you to my sister Char for keeping all things on track and plating the food so beautifully for this book.

FROM ALICIA:

To Tiffany, for her perseverance, dedication to getting it right, and incandescent personality. I am incredibly grateful for the opportunity to spread our wings together. Thank you for indulging my white-plate bias!

To my husband, for his unwavering love, encouragement and enthusiasm.

To our friend, Jon Harris, for igniting this flame.

ADDITIONAL CREDITS:

Makeup: Lorrie Bradshaw **Photography:** Jason Levkulich
Tiffany's Assistant: Charessa Williams

www.ingramcontent.com/pod-product-compliance
Lightning Source LLC
LaVergne TN
LVHW070213110826
845147LV00003B/566

* 9 7 8 1 9 6 8 9 1 9 1 5 3 *